D1474118

Easy Dairy Free Keto Diet Cookbook for Beginners After 50
90 Delicious Low-Carb Recipes to Heal Your Body & Help You Lose Weight

Sandra Grant

3

Introduction

Many attribute pain, malaise, and excess weight to old age. In this book, I will look at the link between aging and health, and also explain. If you have a loved one over the age of 50 or fall into this age category, let's see how ketosis can help everyone enjoy their golden years.

It is much more difficult for a person over 50 to live on unhealthy food than a teenager or 20-year-old whose body is still stable. Therefore, older adults need to eat a more optimal diet, avoid "empty calories" from sugar or foods rich in anti-nutrients such as whole grains, and increase nutrient-rich fats and proteins.

In addition, most of the diet that older adults choose (or presented in hospitals) contains highly processed foods that are poor in nutrients. This includes white bread, pasta, prunes, mashed potatoes, puddings, etc.

The keto diet is absolutely the best choice for our people and long term use. To improve insulin performance, reduce the incidence of cognitive impairment and improve overall health.

Interesting facts about the keto diet

A high-fat diet, or keto diet, is recommended for patients with diabetes, cancer, and Alzheimer's disease. "Fat: a new paradigm for health", under this heading The Research Unit of the Swiss Bank - Research Institute Credit Suisse published a report in September 2015 that dispelled the most persistent myths about the dangers of fat and the benefits of carbohydrates. The report formulates the main principles of the keto diet or nutrition of the LCHF system:

- *you don't get fat from natural fats,*
- *saturated fats are safe for health,*
- *the cause of the obesity epidemic is the excessive consumption of carbohydrates and refined vegetable oils*

What is the keto diet

B ack in the early 60s, the basics of our nutrition began to be made up of such as rice, potatoes, pasta and bread, and nutritionists are in one voice that fatty foods are dangerous to health and lead to obesity. However, more and more research is now emerging that carbohydrates are nowhere near as healthy as we think. In September 2015, Credit Suisse Research Institute published its report "Fat: A New Paradigm for Health", in which it dispelled the most persistent myths and backed up the information with links to research. Impartial employees of the bank worked on the report, interested, first of all, in the most objective data for agents. The most complete debunking of the myth is also reflected in the documentary "Charged with carbohydrates: the culture of killing food."

In connection with the results of new studies, which are more often reported by the world media, the keto diet, or the LCHF nutrition system (an abbreviation for low carbohydrate high fat, "low carbohydrates, high fat") began to gain popularity. So that a person gets more energy from natural fats and proteins: you can generously fill food with vegetable oils - olive, coconut, flaxseed, eat fatty meat and fish, nuts. For example, dark chocolate - 85% or more cocoa content. Fiber and the minimum amount of carbohydrates on this diet can be obtained from vegetables and fruits, but not starchy and sugary - they refuse potatoes, beets and carrots on LCHF. Completely exclude or greatly reduce the amount of cereals, bread and, most importantly, sweets, including sweet fruits. We suggest getting the necessary vitamins on a keto diet from vegetables.

Thus, there should be no more than 50 grams of carbohydrates per day, including all vegetables and fruits, sweeteners, and cereals.

The main advantages of such a diet are the ability to eat your fill at any time, as well as a lot of foods that remain in the diet. In addition, a large amount of fat allows the body to stay hungry for a long time, so 2-3 meals without snacks is enough.

This nutritional system originated in Sweden, which was the first country where official dietetics revised nutritional standards: the Swedish Technology Assessment Council studied 16,000 dietetics studies and concluded that a low-carb and high-fat diet was most effective in combating obesity.

Despite the fact that the ketogenic diet was used in the first half of the twentieth century in the treatment of epilepsy, relatively recently it began to be recommended for other diseases as well. Research in the field is still ongoing, but many foreign nutritionists are practicing it with success.

The importance of keto in old age

P art of aging involves some degree of deterioration in our functions, but it doesn't have to be debilitating and isolating. This is, unfortunately, a sad reality for many older people in our society. The high-carb diet often prescribed to people in this age group does not help either.

Instead of seeing aging as a curse, we can maintain healthier mental and physical health at any age through better nutrition. And the truth is, following a ketogenic diet offers many benefits for older adults:

Insulin resistance. Many older people in our society are overweight and suffer from insulin-related illnesses such as diabetes. This is serious because diabetes can lead to vision loss, kidney disease, and more.

Bone health. Osteoporosis, in which a decrease in bone density causes bones to become brittle and brittle, is one of the most common conditions seen in older men and women. In such cases, doctors advise increasing the calcium in the diet through the daily intake of dairy products. But the fact is, countries with the highest rates of osteoporosis tend to have the highest rates of dairy consumption.

It is much better to focus on a low toxin keto diet that interferes with absorption and is rich in all micronutrients, rather than being overloaded with a specific macronutrient (in this case, calcium).

Inflammation. For many people, aging includes pain from injuries that occurred at a younger age, or joint problems such as arthritis. Ketosis can help reduce the production of substances called cytokines that promote inflammation.

Lack of nutrients. Generally, older adults have higher deficiencies in important nutrients such as:

• *Iron: Deficiency can lead to head fog and distraction.*

• *Vitamin B12: A deficiency can lead to neurological conditions such as dementia.*

• *Fat: Deficiency can lead to skin and vision problems and vitamin deficiencies.*

• *Vitamin D: Deficiency causes cognitive impairment in the elderly, increases the risk of cardiovascular disease, and even contributes to the risk of cancer*

High-quality sources of animal protein in a ketogenic diet can easily make up for deficiencies in these important nutrients.

Blood sugar control

As we said, there is a link between low blood sugar and brain diseases such as Alzheimer's, dementia, and Parkinson's. Some factors that can contribute to Alzheimer's disease:

• *Excessive intake of carbohydrates, especially from fructose, which is sharply reduced on a keto diet.*

• *Lack of dietary fat and cholesterol, which are good for your health and are high in keto.*

• *Oxidative stress that ketosis protects against.*

Not only can a ketogenic diet help improve the response to insulin, but it can also help protect against memory problems that often appear with age.

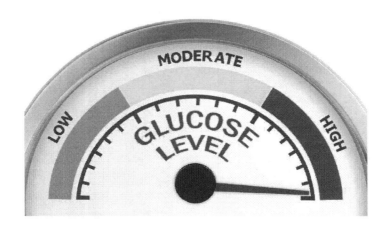

Is it possible to live on a keto diet permanently?

This is a tricky question, and still an open one, especially when it comes to people with conditions like Alzheimer's.

Despite the positive research results, the ketogenic diet should not be taken as a medicine or treatment. Moreover, not every organism is able to easily adapt to it. "With the wrong transition, chronic conditions can worsen, in particular, with inadequate work of the gastrointestinal tract, fermentopathy, stool retention, headaches, and bad breath can occur," nutritiologists warn. - For example, elderly patients with senile dementia may develop diabetes or a pre-diabetic state. Due to the large amount of fat, some of them may start the process of ketoacidosis - a pathological condition during the production of ketone bodies. The state of ketoacidosis is dangerous to health and life. "

That is why it is necessary to apply the keto diet only after consulting a doctor and under the supervision of a specialist.

One of the possible solutions for those who find it difficult to adhere to a diet, scientists consider the development of special nutritional supplements that support healthy ketosis (this is the name of the normal state of the body, in which it receives most of its energy from fat). Work in this direction is already underway. Scientists at the University of California, led by Professor of Neurology Raymond Swenson, managed to recreate the effect of the keto diet using the 2DG (2-deoxyglucose) molecule. The study was conducted in rodents with brain inflammation. As a result of the application of a molecule that stopped glucose metabolism and created a ketogenic state, the level of inflammation dropped dramatically. In other words, scientists are on the way to create a drug that will help achieve the effect without adhering to the strict keto diet.

But no dietary supplement can replace a complete, healthy, balanced diet. They can only be used in conjunction with nutrition, exercise and healthy sleep. To maintain optimal health, including cognitive health, you need to include adequate amounts of the right fat in your diet. The following macro and microelements are necessary for mental health: omega 3, vitamin D, vitamin C, resveratrol, probiotics, magnesium, etc. It is ideal to obtain these substances from food, but if there are any deficient conditions, then it is necessary to add supplements.

Breakfast

<u>Coconut Milk Pancakes</u>

⏱ Cook Time:15		🍳 Serving:4			
🥞 Fat:35g		🍰 Carbogydrates:15g	☺ Protein:16.2g	©	Calori es:442

Ingredients

Dry Ingredients

- 6 tablespoon coconut flour
- 4 tablespoon granulated sweetener
- 1 teaspoon baking powder

Wet Ingredients

- 6 tablespoon unsweetened coconut milk
- 4 large eggs
- 2 teaspoon vanilla extract

Instructions

1. In a mixing bowl add all of the dry ingredients
2. In a seperate bowl mix together coconut milk, eggs and vanilla extract. Be sure to shake can before opening
3. Preheat skillet or pan on medium heat for cooking and add coconut oil or butter
4. Combine dry and wet and beat well with a whisk until batter is smooth and free of lumps
5. Add to pan and cook each side evenly. If cooking too fast pull off heat and lower temperature. Pancakes should be fluffy and not runnny on the inside but golden brown on the outside.

Keto Breakfast Dairy-free Smoothie Bowl

⏲ Cook Time:10 min	🥄 Serving:3			
🍲 Fat:45g	🍰 Carbogydrates:10 g	🥛 Protein:22.2g	©	Calories:642

Ingredients

- 1 ½ cups (350 ml) full-fat coconut milk
- 1 cup (110 g) frozen raspberries
- ¼ cup (60 ml) MCT oil or melted coconut oil, or ¼ cup (40 g) unflavored MCT oil powder
- ¼ cup (40 g) collagen peptides or protein powder
- 2 tablespoons chia seeds
- 1 tablespoon apple cider vinegar
- 1 teaspoon vanilla extract
- 1 tablespoon erythritol, or 4 drops liquid stevia

Toppings (optional)

- Unsweetened shredded coconut
- Hulled hemp seeds
- Fresh berries of choice

Instructions

1. Place all the pudding ingredients in a blender or food processor and blend until smooth. Serve in bowls with your favorite toppings, if desired.

20

Keto Breakfast Casserole

⏱	Cook Time:70 min	👥	Serving:10				
🍲	Fat:15g	🍰	Carbogydrates:4g	💧 Protein:13g	©		Calories:200

Ingredients

- 1 Tbsp garlic, minced
- 1 lb breakfast sausage
- 12 eggs
- ½ cup almond milk
- 2 tsp mustard powder
- 1 tsp oregano
- ¼ tsp salt
- pepper, to taste
- 1½ cups broccoli florets
- 1 zucchini, diced
- 1 red bell pepper, diced
- (or 3-4 cups veggies of choice)

- drizzle of oil
- ½ cup onion

Instructions

1. Preheat oven to 375°F (190°C).
2. In a skillet over medium heat, add a drizzle of oil and sauté onion and garlic.
3. Once transparent, add sausage and cook until browned, 7-10 minutes.
4. Add to a 13×9-inch casserole or baking dish and set aside.
5. In a large bowl, whisk together eggs, milk of choice, and seasonings. Stir in chopped veggies.
6. Pour mixture over sausage.
7. Bake until firm and cooked through, 30-40 minutes.
8. Allow to cool slightly before slicing into squares, serving, and enjoying!
9. Store leftovers in the fridge for up to 5 days, and reheat individual portions in the microwave.

Crispy Keto Corned Beef & Radish Hash

⏱ Cook Time:10 min	🍴 Serving:2			
🥩 Fat:16g	🍱 Carbogydrates:1.5g	🥄 Protein:23g	© Calories:252

Ingredients

- 2 tbsp olive oil
- 1/2 cup diced onions
- 2 cup radishes, diced to about 1/2 inch
- 1 tsp kosher salt
- 1/2 tsp ground black pepper
- 1 tsp dried oregano (Mexican if you have it)
- 1/2 tsp garlic powder
- 2 twelve oz can corned beef or 2 cup finely chopped corned beef, packed

Instructions

1. Heat the olive oil in a large saute pan and add the onions, radishes, salt and pepper.

2. Saute the onions and radishes on medium heat for 5 minutes or until softened.

3. Add the oregano, garlic powder, and corned beef to the pan and stir well until combined.

4. Cook over low to medium heat, stirring occasionally for 10 minutes or until the radishes are soft and starting to brown.

5. Press the mixture into the bottom of the pan and cook on high heat for 2-3 minutes or until the bottom is crisp and brown.

6. Serve hot.

Coconut Flour Porridge

⏱ Cook Time:7 min	🍳 Serving:1			
🍥 Fat:28.5g	🍰 Carbogydrates:13g	☕ Protein:13g	© Calories:345

Ingredients

- 2 tablespoons coconut flour
- 2 tablespoons golden flax meal
- 3/4 cup water
- pinch of salt
- 1 large egg beaten
- 2 teaspoons butter or ghee
- 1 tablespoon heavy cream or coconut milk
- 1 tablespoon low carb brown sugar or your favorite sweetener

Instructions

1. Measure the first four ingredients into a small pot over medium heat and stir. When it begins to simmer, turn it down to medium-low and whisk until it begins to thicken.
2. Remove the coconut flour porridge from heat and add the beaten egg, a half at a time, while whisking continuously. Place back on the heat and continue to whisk until the porridge thickens.
3. Remove from the heat and continue to whisk for about 30 seconds before adding the butter, cream and sweetener.
4. Garnish with your favorite toppings. (4 grams net carbs)

Grilled Chicken Salad

⏱ Cook Time:35 min	🍴 Serving:6				
🥧 Fat:34g	🍞 Carbogydrates:5g	☺ Protein:21g	© Calories:415		

Ingredients

For the grilled chicken blt salad:

- 1-1.5 lbs boneless skinless chicken breasts pounded to even thickness
- 1 medium avocado
- 8 slices bacon sugar-free for Whole30, cooked until crisp, drained, and crumbled
- reserved bacon fat to brush chicken and grill
- sea salt ground peppercorn and onion powder to sprinkle on chicken
- 1 5 oz container salad greens or the equivalent of your favorite greens
- 1 small container cherry tomatoes cut in half
- peppercorn ranch dressing as much as desired

For the peppercorn ranch

- 1/2 cup homemade mayo or purchase Paleo friendly mayo
- 1/4 cup coconut milk blended (water and cream)
- 1 tsp lemon juice
- 3 drops hot sauce about 1/8 tsp adjust to taste
- 1/4 tsp sea salt
- 1 clove garlic minced
- 2 scallions thinly sliced
- 1 tsp ground tricolor peppercorns

Instructions

1. Make the dressing first: Blend all dressing ingredients either using an immersion blender or in a standard blender, set aside or chill until ready to use

24

2. Now, cook the bacon first and set aside, reserving bacon fat to brush on the grill (or cast iron skillet) and chicken
3. Generously brush the chicken and grill with bacon fat and sprinkle with salt, pepper, and onion powder. Grill on both sides, flipping once, until just done, then remove to a plate and cover loosely with aluminum foil
4. To assemble the salad, begin with the greens and add the cherry tomatoes, cooked crumbled bacon, then cut open the avocado and slice it thinly; arrange on the salad as desired.
5. Slice the chicken breast thin and arrange on salad. Once ready to serve, drizzle on ranch dressing (you'll have extra) and gently toss/mix to coat. Serves 4-6. Enjoy! Store extra dressing in a tightly covered container in the refrigerator for up to 1 week.

Shrimp and Avocado Salad

⏲ Cook Time:20 min	🍽 Serving:1				
🥩 Fat:18.5g	🍞 Carbogydrates:9g	☺ Protein:19g	© Calories:265

Ingredients

- 1 lb. cooked frozen shrimp, thawed (see notes)
- 2 avocados, diced
- 3 T fresh-squeezed lime juice
- 1 tsp. ground cumin (or less if you're not a big cumin fan)
- 1/2 tsp. finely ground sea salt
- 3 T extra-virgin olive oil
- 6 green onions, thickly sliced

Instructions

1. Let shrimp thaw overnight in the fridge (or you can thaw them in the bag in cold water in the sink if you forget to plan ahead.)

2. Put thawed shrimp into a colander placed in the sink and let the shrimp drain well. (If you're in a hurry, drain shrimp and pat dry with paper towels.

3. Whisk together the lime juice, cumin, and salt, then whisk in the olive oil a little at a time to make the dressing.

4. Cut up the avocado into bite-sized chunks, put in a bowl large enough to hold all the ingredients, and toss with about half the dressing.

5. Cut the green onions into thick slices.

6. If the shrimp is still wet, pat dry with paper towels.

7. Add the green onions and drained shrimp to the avocados and gently combine, adding as much additional dressing as you prefer.

8. Season to taste with more salt if desired

Easy Shakshuka

⏱	Cook Time:35 min	🍳	Serving:6				
🍲	Fat:12.8g	🍞	Carbogydrates:16.6g	🥄 Protein:11.2g	©	Calories:216	

Ingredients

- 2 tablespoon olive oil
- 1 large yellow onion, chopped
- 1 large red bell pepper or roasted red bell pepper, chopped
- 1/4 teaspoon fine sea salt
- 3 cloves garlic, pressed or minced
- 2 tablespoon tomato paste
- 1 teaspoon ground cumin
- 1/2 teaspoon smoked paprika
- 1/4 teaspoon red pepper flakes, reduce or omit if sensitive to spice
- 1 large can (28 ounce) crushed tomatoes, preferably fire-roasted
- 2 tablespoon chopped fresh cilantro or flat-leaf parsley, plus addition cilantro or parsley leaves for garnish
- Freshly ground black pepper, to taste
- 5 to 6 large eggs

Instructions

1. Preheat the oven to 375 degrees Fahrenheit. Warm the oil in a large, oven-safe skillet (preferably stainless steel) over medium heat. Once shimmering, add the onion, bell pepper, and salt. Cook, stirring often, until the onions are tender and turning translucent, about 4 to 6 minutes.

2. Add the garlic, tomato paste, cumin, paprika and red pepper flakes. Cook, stirring constantly, until nice and fragrant, 1 to 2 minutes.

3. Pour in the crushed tomatoes with their juices and add the cilantro. Stir, and let the mixture come to a simmer. Reduce

the heat as necessary to maintain a gentle simmer, and cook for 5 minutes to give the flavors time to meld.

4. Turn off the heat. Taste (careful, it's hot), and add salt and pepper as necessary. Use the back of a spoon to make a well near the perimeter and crack the egg directly into it. Gently spoon a bit of the tomato mixture over the whites to help contain the egg. Repeat with the remaining 4 to 5 eggs, depending on how many you can fit. Sprinkle a little salt and pepper over the eggs.

5. Carefully transfer the skillet to the oven (it's heavy) and bake for 8 to 12 minutes, checking often once you reach 8 minutes. They're done when the egg whites are an opaque white and the yolks have risen a bit but are still soft. They should still jiggle in the centers when you shimmy the pan. (Keep in mind that they'll continue cooking after you pull the dish out of the oven.)

Avocado Omelette

⏱ Cook Time:5 min	🍳 Serving:2				
🍲 Fat:23g	🧁 Carbogydrates:11g	😊 Protein:16g	©	Calories:310

Ingredients

- •3 eggs, lightly beaten
- •3 Tbsp. almond milk
- •As needed   Nonstick cooking spray
- •1/2 cup Tofu cheese
- •1 Tbsp. sliced green onion
- •1/4 cup chopped red bell pepper

•1 ripe, Fresh California Avocado, seeded, peeled and cubed

Instructions

1. Mix eggs and milk.
2. Spray a large skillet with nonstick cooking spray and heat over medium low heat. Pour egg mixture into skillet. Cook eggs until top is almost set.
3. Sprinkle with cheese and green onion. Cook, about 2 minutes.
4. Top with red pepper and avocado, fold over and serve immediately.

Serving Suggestion: For a tasty brunch serve with a fresh fruit salad on the side.

Dairy Free Frittata

⏱	Cook Time:50 min	🍳	Serving:6				
🍲	Fat:9g	🍰	Carbogydrates:5g	🥚	Protein:11g	©	Calories:143

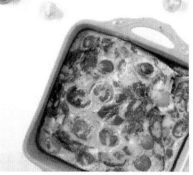

Ingredients

FOR THE VEGGIES:

- •1 tablespoon olive oil
- •½ of a medium red onion, chopped
- •1 large red bell pepper, chopped
- •¼ teaspoon fine sea salt
- •3 cloves garlic, minced
- •1 (5 ounce) package fresh baby spinach leaves
- •⅓ to ½ cup sun-dried tomatoes, patted dry and chopped (to taste)*

FOR THE EGG BASE:

- •12 large eggs
- •⅓ cup unsweetened plain almond milk
- •½ teaspoon fine sea salt
- •¼ teaspoon pepper

Instructions

Preheat the oven to 350°F. Generously grease a 9x13 inch baking dish with nonstick spray and set aside.

FOR THE VEGGIES:

1. Add the olive oil to a large skillet set over medium heat. When hot, add in the onion, bell pepper and salt and cook for about 5 to 7 minutes, until tender. Stir in the garlic and cook for 30 seconds, until fragrant.
2. Working in batches, add in the spinach and cook until wilted. Remove from the heat, then stir in the sun-dried tomatoes. Taste and season with additional salt as needed.

FOR THE EGG BASE:

1. In a medium-large bowl, whisk together the eggs, milk, salt and pepper until well combined and smooth.
2. Transfer the veggie mixture to the prepared baking dish and spread evenly, then pour the egg mixture over the top.
3. Bake for about 25 to 30 minutes, until the eggs are cooked through, set and appear puffed (the center should also only jiggle just a tad if you give it a gentle shake).
4. Remove from the oven and let cool for about 10 minutes before digging in. If you run a butter knife gently around the edges, the egg slab will release easier from the pan.

Keto Cacao Coconut Granola

⏱ Cook Time:30 min	🍳 Serving:3				
🍰 Fat:6g	🍞 Carbogydrates:7g	☺ Protein:7g	© Calories:112		

Ingredients

- 1/4 cup cacao nibs
- 1/4 cup chopped raw walnuts
- 1/4 cup sesame seeds
- 1/4 cup sugar-free vanilla flavored protein
- powder
- 3 tablespoons granulated erythritol
- 1 teaspoon ground cinnamon
- 1/8 teaspoon kosher salt
- 1/3 cup coconut oil
- 1 large egg white, beaten

- 1/2 cup chopped raw pecans
- 1/2 cup flax seeds
- 1/2 cup superfine blanched almond flour
- 1/2 cup unsweetened dried coconut

Instructions

1. Preheat the oven to 300F
2. Line a 15x10" sheet pan with parchment paper.
3. Stir all of the ingredients until the mixture is
4. crumbly and holds together in small clumps.
5. Spread out on the parchment-lined pan. Bake
6. for ~30 minutes or until golden brown and fragrant (oven times may vary).
7. Let the granola cool completely in the pan before removing. Store in an airtight container in
8. the refrigerator for up to 2 weeks.

Sausage Egg Casserole

⏱	Cook Time:60 min	🐾	Serving:8				
🍖	Fat:16g	🧀	Carbogydrates:7g	☺	Protein:15g	©	Calories:230

Ingredients

- 1 tbs dried sage
- 1 tbs dried thyme
- 1 tbs dried rosemary ½ tsp nutmeg
- 2 tsp dried parsley
- 1 tsp paprika
- ¼ tsp cayenne
- 1 tsp black pepper
- 10 eggs
- ½ cup coconut milk

- 1 medium spaghetti squash
- 2 lbs ground chicken, turkey, or pork
- 1 medium sweet onion, chopped
- 1½ tbs sea salt

Instructions

1. Preheat over to 375 degrees
2. Grease a 9x13 pan with coconut oil
3. Cut spaghetti squash in half lengthwise and scrape out the seeds
4. Place squash cut side down on baking sheet and bake for 40 -45 minutes until easily pierced with a fork
5. Meanwhile, add ground turkey and onion to a large skillet over medium heat and cook untilmeat is browned
6. Add seasonings and mix to combine
7. Add eggs and coconut milk to a mixing bowl and whisk until combined

8. When spaghetti squash is finished cooking, reduce oven temperature to 350 degrees
9. Let squash cool and then scrape the insides out with a large fork into greased baking dish
10. Spread the meat mixture on top of squash in pan
11. Pour the egg mixture evenly on top of meat and squash
12. Mix slightly to ensure the egg mixture is spread throughout the pan
13. Bake for 50-60 minutes until slightly browned and the casserole bounces back when pressed on.

Pulled Pork Breakfast Keto Hash

⏱	Cook Time:15 min	🍴	Serving:2				
🍖	Fat:18g	🧺	Carbogydrates:6g	😊	Protein:12g	©	Calories:280

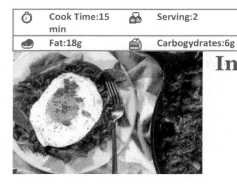

Ingredients

- 2 tablespoons FOC (fat of choice)
- 1 turnip, diced
- 1/2 teaspoon paprika
- 1/4 tsp salt & 1/4 tsp black pepper
- 1/4 teaspoon garlic powder
- 3 Brussels sprouts, halved
- 1 cup chopped kale
- 2 tablespoons diced red onion
- 3 ounces pulled pork (or meat of choice)
- 2 eggs

Instructions

1. Heat the oil in a large cast iron skillet over medium high heat. Add the diced turnips and the spices to the skillet. Cook 5 minutes stirring occasionally.

2. Add the remaining vegetables to the skillet and cook another 2-3 minutes until they start to soften. Add in the pork and cook 2 minutes.

3. Make 2 divots in the hash and crack in two eggs. Cover and cook 3-5 minutes just until the whites are set.

Keto Breakfast "Potatoes"

⏱ Cook Time:20 min	🐮 Serving:4				
🍲 Fat:16g	🍰 Carbogydrates:7g	☺ Protein:5g	© Calories:230		

Ingredients

- •1 large turnip, peeled and diced (270g)
- •1/4 onion, diced (56g)
- •3 slices bacon
- •1 tablespoon olive oil
- •1/2 teaspoon each of paprika, garlic powder,
- •salt, and pepper
- •1 green onion, sliced, for garnish
- •Parsley, for garnish

Instructions

1. Add the oil to a large skillet over medium high heat. Add in the turnips and spices. Cook 5-7 minutes stirring occasionally.
2. Add in the onion and cook 3 minutes until it starts to soften. Chop the bacon into small pieces and add to the skillet. Continue to cook another 5-7 minutes until the bacon is crispy.
3. Sprinkle with green onion and parsley to serve.

Avocado Buns Breakfast Burger

⏱	Cook Time:10 min	🍴	Serving:1				
🍲	Fat:10g	🍞	Carbogydrates:3g	☺	Protein:8g	©	Calories:230

Ingredients

- 1 ripe avocado
- 1 egg
- 2 thin slices of bacon
- 1 red onion slice
- 1 tomato slice
- 1 lettuce leaf
- 1 tbs keto-friendly mayonnaise
- Sea salt, to taste
- Sesame seeds, for garnish

Instructions

1. Place the bacon slices on a cold frying pan. Turn the stove on and start frying the bacon. When bacon beings to curl, flip it with a fork. Continue cooking the bacon until it is crispy.
2. Remove the bacon from the pan and crack the egg into the same pan, using the bacon fat to cook it. Cook until the white is set but the yolk is still runny.
3. Slice the avocados in half width-wise. Remove the pit and use a spoon to scoop it out of its skin.
4. Fill the hole where the pit used to be with mayonnaise.
5. Layer with lettuce, tomato, onion, bacon, and fried egg.
6. Season with sea salt.
7. Top with the second half of the avocado.
8. Sprinkle with sesame seeds.

Steak and Eggs

⏱ Cook Time:15 min	🎲 Serving:1			
🍲 Fat:36g	🍰 Carbogydrates:3g	😊 Protein44g	© Calories:510

Ingredients

- 1 tbsp butter
- 3 eggs
- 4 oz. sirloin
- 1/4 avocado
- Salt
- Pepper

Instructions

Melt your butter in a pan and fry 2-3 eggs until the whites are set and yolk is to desired doneness. Season with salt and pepper.

In another pan, cook your sirloin (or favorite cut of steak) until desired doneness. Then slice into bite sized strips and season with salt and pepper.

Slice up some avocado and serve together!

Fish and Seafood Dishes

Fish Fingers

⏱	Cook Time:15 min	🍴	Serving:4			
🥩	Fat:40g	🍰	Carbogydrates:3g	🥤 Protein:30g	©	Calories:295

Ingredients

- 250 g white fish such as cod, cut into slices (8.8 ounces)
- 1 large egg, lightly beaten
- 1/3 cup almond flour (33 g/1.2 ounces)
- 1/2 teaspoon sea salt
- 1/2 teaspoon onion powder
- 1/4 teaspoon garlic powder
- 1/4 teaspoon paprika
- 1/4 cup mayonnaise (55 g/1.9 ounces)
- 1 1/2 tablespoon chimichurri (23 g/0.8 ounces)

Homemade Chimichurri Sauce

- 1 large bunch fresh parsley (60 g/2.1 ounces)
- 1/4 cup fresh oregano (15 g/0.5 ounces)
- 4 cloves garlic, chopped
- 1 small red chile pepper, seeds removed
- 2 tablespoons apple cider vinegar or fresh lime juice (30 ml)
- 1/2 cup extra-virgin olive oil (120 ml/4 fl ounces)
- 1/2 teaspoon salt
- 1/4 teaspoon black pepper

Instructions

1. Preheat oven to 210 °C/ 410 °F. Beat egg in a small, shallow bowl. To create the "breading," mix dry ingredients in another shallow bowl or plate.
2. Cut fish fillets into "fingers" about an inch (2.5 cm) wide.

39

3. Line and grease a baking tray. Place the fish in the egg, coating all sides, and then transfer to the almond meal mix, and toss to cover. Shake off excess breading.
4. Place on the tray, and continue with remaining fish. Bake 6-8 minutes and then turn, and bake another 5 minutes, or until golden-brown.
5. To make the chimichurri, place all the ingredients in a blender and process until smooth.
6. To make the chimichurri mayo, combine mayo and chimichurri together in a small bowl. The leftover chimichurri can be refrigerated in an airtight container for up to 1 week.
7. Serve the fish fingers immediately with the mayo and wedges of lemon. Optionally, serve with a bowl of dressed greens.

Shrimp Avocado Salad

⏱	Cook Time:5 min	🍴	Serving:2				
🍤	Fat:33g	🍰	Carbogydrates:12g	☕	Protein:24g	©	Calories:430

Ingredients

- 8 ounces shrimp peeled, deveined, patted dry
- 1 large avocado, diced
- 1 small beefsteak tomato, diced and drained
- 1/3 cup crumbled feta cheese
- 1/3 cup freshly chopped cilantro or parsley
- 2 tablespoons salted butter, melted
- 1 tablespoon lemon juice
- 1 tablespoon olive oil
- 1/4 teaspoon salt
- 1/4 teaspoon black pepper

Instructions

1. Toss shrimp with melted butter in a bowl until well-coated.
2. Heat a pan over medium-high heat for a few minutes until hot. Add shrimp to the pan in a single layer, searing for a minute or until it starts to become pink around the edges, then flip and cook until shrimp are cooked through, less than a minute.
3. Transfer the shrimp to a plate as they finish cooking. Let them cool while you prepare the other ingredients.
4. Add all other ingredients to a large mixing bowl -- diced avocado, diced tomato, feta cheese, cilantro, lemon juice, olive oil, salt, and pepper -- and toss to mix.
5. Add shrimp and stir to mix together. Add additional salt and pepper, to taste.

41

Avocado Lime Salmon

⏱ Cook Time:30 min	🍳 Serving:2					
🥩 Fat:44g	🍰 Carbogydrates:12g	💧 Protein:36g	© Calories:570			

Ingredients

- 100 grams chopped cauliflower
- 1 large avocado
- 1 tablespoon fresh lime juice
- 2 tablespoons diced red onion
- 2 tablespoons olive oil
- 2 (6-ounce) boneless salmon fillets
- Salt and pepper

Instructions

1. Melt your butter in a pan and fry 2-3 eggs until the whites are set and yolk is to desired doneness. Season Place the cauliflower in a food processor and pulse into rice-like grains.

2. Grease a skillet with cooking spray and heat over medium heat.

3. Add the cauliflower rice and cook, covered, for 8 minutes until tender. Set aside.

4. Combine the avocado, lime juice, and red onion in a food processor and blend smooth.

5. Heat the oil in a large skillet over medium-high heat.

6. Season the salmon with salt and pepper, then add to the skillet skin-side down.

7. Cook for 4 to 5 minutes until seared, then flip and cook for another 4 to 5 minutes.

8. Serve the salmon over a bed of cauliflower rice topped with the avocado cream.

Broccoli and Shrimp Sautéed in Butter

⏱	Cook Time:15 min	🦐	Serving:2						
🍳	Fat:14g	🍞	Carbogydrates:5g	🥑	Protein:30g	©	Calories:277		

Ingredients

- 1 cup broccoli, cut into small pieces
- 1 clove garlic, crushed
- 300 g shrimp, cleaned
- 2 tbsp butter
- 1 tsp lemon juice
- Salt, to taste

Instructions

1. Chop the broccoli into small portions or whichever size you prefer, but smaller pieces cook faster.
2. Melt the butter in a preheated pan. Gently toss in the chopped broccoli and crushed garlic when the butter becomes hot (but not smoking). Stir to cook.
3. Leave over the heat for 3-4 minutes. Stir from time to time.
4. Clean the shrimp before adding them to the pan. Let it cook for around 3-4 minutes.
5. Once the shrimp turns pink and opaque, drizzle the lemon juice all over.
6. Transfer to a plate and serve.

Keto Calamari

⏱ Cook Time:30 min	🍴 Serving:4			
🍲 Fat:15g	🍰 Carbogydrates:11g	😋 Protein:22g	© Calories:286	

Ingredients

- 1

lb fresh squid cleaned
- 1 egg beaten
- 1/2 cup coconut flour
- 1 teaspoon salt
- 1 teaspoon paprika
- 1/2 teaspoon garlic powder

- 1/2 teaspoon onion powder
- Coconut oil for frying (about 1/4 cup)
- Minced cilantro optional
- Sliced Fresno chili optional
- Squeeze of lime optional
- Harissa Mayo
- 1/4 cup mayonnaise
- 1 tablespoon prepared hariss

Instructions

9. In a small bowl beat the egg. In another bowl combine the coconut flour and spices.
10. Pat the squid dry and dip into the beaten egg then dredge through the flour mixture.
11. Heat the oil in a 10" or larger cast-iron skillet over medium-high heat.
12. Frying in batches making sure to not overcrowd the skillet, fry 2 minutes per side until golden and crisp. Drain on paper towels
13. Either serve as is or toss with cilantro, chilis, and lime and serve with the harissa mayo.

Calamari Stuffed with Pancetta and Vegetables

⏱ Cook Time:20 min	🍲 Serving:4					
🍳 Fat:35g	🍞 Carbogydrates:10.6g	💧 Protein:24g	© Calories:456			

Ingredients

- 40 g (1/4 cup) carrots grated
- 8 g (1 tbsp) garlic grated
- 80 g (3/4 cup) celery diced into very small pieces
- 100 g (1 cup, or one bulb) fennel bulb diced into very small pieces
- 1/2 g (1/2 tsp) thyme powder
- 1-2 bunches fresh rosemary
- 6 g (1 tsp) salt
- 2 g (1 tsp) black pepper

Other

- 14 g (1 tbsp) olive oil drizzling over prepared stuffed squid
- 15 g (1 tbsp) lemon juice freshly squeezed

- 500 g (8 large or 12 16 smaller) squid cleaned
- 82 g (1/2 cup) keto bun center only diced into very small pieces

Stuffing

- 70 g (3 oz) pancetta or pork belly chopped into very small pieces
- 42 g (3 tbsp) of olive oil for grilling
- 68 g (5 tbsp) olive oil for stuffing

Instructions

1. Clean your squid or purchase cleaned squid with tentacles. Rinse under cold running water and set aside
2. Prepare and weigh your vegetables: grate the carrots, onion and garlic. Chop the celery and fennel bulb into very small pieces

45

3. Cut the pancetta or pork belly and the squid arms into thin strips and then chop into very small pieces

4. Heat a grilling pan and add 3 tbsp of olive oil. When oil is sizzling add the pancetta/pork belly and squid arms, carrots, celery, fennel, onion and garlic. Place the fresh bunch of rosemary into the pan. Season with salt. Stir and cook on low heat until the vegetables are translucent, and the pancetta/pork belly is done (but not crispy). Remove the rosemary and discard

5. When stuffing is done, place into a mixing bowl and add 2 tbsp of olive oil and the pepper. Toss to combine

6. Use a teaspoon to insert the stuffing into each squid. Quantity of stuffing needed per squid will depend on the size of your squid. Do not overstuff as the squid will shrink as it cooks. Use a toothpick to seal the opening

7. Heat up the grill pan, and add the olive oil. Reduce heat to low and lay your stuffed squid perpendicular to the grill ridges. Cook for 5-6 minutes on the first side then flip and cook 5-6 minutes on the other side. Remove from heat and place on a platter

8. Finish by drizzling the tablespoon of fresh lemon juice on top and then the tablespoon of olive oil. Garnish with the fennel leaves and a wedge of lemon. Enjoy!

Keto Coconut Shrimp

🕐	Cook Time:30 min	🍴	Serving:4				
🍤	Fat:46g	🏭	Carbogydrates:9g	🥛 Protein:30g	©	Calories:554

Ingredients

•1

lb shrimp peeled with tails left on and deveined

•1 large egg

•1 tablespoon whey protein isolate

•1 cup Bob's Red Mill Unsweetened Shredded Coconut

•3 tablespoons Bob's Red Mill Coconut Flour

•1 tablespoon powdered erythritol

•1 pinch sea salt

•¼ teaspoon paprika

•½ cup coconut oil

Instructions

1. In a medium bowl, whisk the egg and they whey protein isolate together.
2. In another medium bowl, combine the coconut, coconut flour, powdered erythritol, salt and paprika.
3. Butterfly the shrimp by slicing down the back of them until they open up and could almost lay flat.
4. Melt the coconut oil in a large cast iron skillet over medium high heat.
5. Dip the shrimp into the egg wash, let the excess fall off, then dredge through the coconut mixture.
6. In batches, so the pan isn't overcrowded, fry the shrimp for 2-3 minutes per side until golden brown and crispy.
7. Transfer cooked shrimp to a paper towel lined plate to drain excess oil.

Salmon with Garlic Lemon Butter Sauce

⏱	Cook Time:20 min	🍳	Serving:4				
🍪	Fat:21g	🧀	Carbogydrates:2g	☺	Protein:34g	©	Calories:347

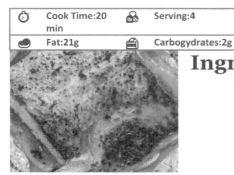

Ingredients

- 4 (6 oz) skinless salmon fillets (about 1-inch thick)
- Salt and freshly ground black pepper
- 2 tsp olive oil
- 2 garlic cloves, minced
- 1/4 cup low-sodium chicken broth
- 2 Tbsp fresh lemon juice
- 3 Tbsp + 1 tsp unsalted butter, diced into 1 Tbsp pieces
- 1/2 tsp honey
- 2 Tbsp minced fresh parsley
- Lemon slices for garnish (optional)

Instructions

1. Remove salmon fillets from refrigerator and allow to rest at room temperature 10 minutes.
2. Meanwhile, prepare the garlic lemon butter sauce. In a small saucepan, melt 1 tsp butter over medium heat.
3. Add garlic and saute until lightly golden brown, about 1 - 2 minutes. Pour in chicken broth and lemon juice.
4. Let sauce simmer until it has reduced by half (to about 3 Tbsp), about 3 minutes. Stir in butter and honey and whisk until combined, set sauce aside.
5. Dab both sides of salmon dry with paper towels, season both sides with salt and pepper.
6. Heat olive oil in a (heavy) 12-inch non-stick skillet over medium-high heat.
7. Once oil is shimmering add salmon and cook about 4 minutes on the first side until golden brown on

48

bottom then flip and cook salmon on opposite side until salmon has cooked through, about 2 - 3 minutes longer.

8. Plate salmon (leaving oil in pan) and drizzle each serving generously with butter sauce, sprinkle with parsley and garnish with lemon slices if desired. Serve immediately.

Low Carb Almond Crusted Cod

⏱	Cook Time:25 min	⚖	Serving:4				
🍴	Fat:13g	🍱	Carbogydrates:4g	☺	Protein:23g	©	Calories:219

Ingredients

- •1 4 filets cod or other white fish
- •1 med lemon zested and juiced
- •1/2 cup crushed almonds can use a food processor or blender to crush
- •1 Tbsp dill either fresh
- •1 Tbsp olive oil
- •salt & pepper to taste
- •1 tsp mild to med. chili spice optional
- •4 tsp Dijon mustard more if you like mustard

Instructions

1. Preheat oven to 400 degrees F. Prepare a baking sheet with either parchment paper laid on top or spray with cooking spray
2. Place cod filets on paper towels to drain of water and pat dry. Place on baking sheet.
3. In a small bowl, combine the lemon zest, lemon juice, crushed almonds, dill, oil, salt and pepper and chili spice if using.
4. Spread each cod filet with a tsp or so of Dijon mustard,smoothing it over the entire top of the filet.

49

Divide the almond mixture among the 4 filets, pressing it evely into the mustard with your hands.

5. Bake the fish until opaue at the thickest part, about 7 minutes for most.cod filets (less time for thin filets).

6. Serve with a green vegetable and lemon slices for a great low carb or keto fish dinner.

Spicy Fish Cakes with 2 Dipping Sauces

⏱	Cook Time:25 min	🍴	Serving:4				
🍽	Fat:16g	🧳	Carbogydrates:9g	🥄	Protein:42g	©	Calories:358

Ingredients

- squeeze of fresh lime juice I used juice from 1/2 medium lime (2-3 wedges)
- 1/4 tsp fish sauce
- 3/4 cup Panko crumbs *note: not slow carb compliant

Tartar Sauce

- 1 cup mayonnaise olive oil based
- 3 Tbsp capers
- 3 Tbsp fresh lemon juice
- 2 Tbsp chopped dill pickles finely chopped
- 1 Tbsp chopped scallions
- 1/4 tsp black pepper

Spicy Dipping Sauce

- 1-2 Tbsp fish sauce provides salty umami
- 1 Tbsp rice wine vinegar more mellow than other vinegars
- 1 Tbsp fresh lime juice juice from 1/2 lime
- 1 Tbsp ground coriander
- 1 tsp chopped green chile pepper

- 2 Tbsp Refined olive oil refined olive oil has higher smoke point than extra virgin
- 2 lbs. skinless fish filets
- 2 large eggs
- 3 Tbsp scallions sliced thinly on an angle
- 3 Tbsp Italian parsley leaves chopped
- 2 tsp sea salt
- 1/2 tsp freshly ground black pepper
- 1 Tbsp grated fresh ginger
- 1/4 tsp ground coriander
- 1 tsp chipotle powder (or any spicy chile powder)

Instructions

1. Preheat oven to 200 degrees F
2. Combine all ingredients in large bowl and mash together with fork or hands until well blended (alternatively, you

can combine in blender fitted with blade attachment and just pulse lightly about 5 pulses – do not overblend!). What you are aiming for is a mixture of small, medium and large chunks of fish.

3. Using your hands, form small balls of the fish mixture into patties about 1/2 inch thick and about 2-3 inches in diameter (about 1/3 cup each).

4. Heat 2 Tbsp oil in large skillet (cast iron if you have it), until lightly smoking (about 3 minutes). Place patties in skillet starting at 6:00 direction and moving clockwise, so you remember which ones to turn over first. Do not crowd the patties; leave a little room between each one.

5. Cook patties until browned and crispy on one side (about 5 minutes). Do not move them around while they are browning. Flip, starting at the 6:00 fish cake, and brown about 3 minutes or less on the other side

6. Remove the fish cakes to a baking sheet and place in oven to keep warm. Add more oil to skillet if needed and repeat process with remaining patties.

Recipe for Mexican Fish Stew

⏱	Cook Time:30 min	🍽	Serving:6			
🍲	Fat:7g	🏛	Carbogydrates:8g	Protein:19g	©	Calories:196

Ingredients

- 2 Tbsp olive oil
- 1 med onion chopped
- 1 large carrot sliced thinly
- 3 med celery stalks sliced thinly
- 3-6 cloves garlic smashed or minced
- 1 tsp smoky pepper blend
- 1/2 tsp dried thyme
- 1 cup white wine
- 4 cups chicken broth
- 1/2 cup chopped cilantro
- 2 14 oz cans Rotel diced tomatoes
- 1/2 tsp salt
- 3 leaves bay
- 6 oz scallops
- 7 oz walleye, coarsely chopped
- 1 lb mussels
- 3 oz white fish, coarsely chopped
- 2 med limes, cut into wedges optional
- 1 med lemon, sliced for garnish

Instructions

1. Heat oil over med-high heat in a dutch oven or large pot. Saute onion, carrot and celery in oil for 3-5 minutes until translucent. Add smashed garlic and cook for 1 more minute
2. Add spices and stir in to the onion mixture to coat. Add wine, broth, cilantro, and tomatoes to pot and simmer together for 15-20 minutes over medium heat. Add salt to taste.
3. Add all fish to the pot and cook, covered for about 5 minutes or until mussels open and white fish is opaque.
4. Add sliced lemons to the pot and serve.
5. Optional: serve with lime wedges that people can squeeze into the soup.

53

Keto Thai fish curry

⏱ Cook Time:30 min	🍳 Serving:4				
🍤 Fat:18g	🏠 Carbogydrates:4g	🥗 Protein:23g	© Calories:244		

Ingredients

- 1 tbsp coconut oil for greasing the baking dish
- 1½ lbs salmon, boneless fillets or white fish, in pieces
- salt and pepper
- 1 oz. butter or ghee
- 2 tbsp red curry paste or green curry paste
- 2 cups coconut cream
- ½ cup (¼ oz.) fresh cilantro, chopped
- 1 lb cauliflower or broccoli

Instructions

1. Preheat the oven to 400°F (200°C). Grease a medium-sized baking dish.
2. Place the fish pieces snuggly in the baking dish. Salt and pepper generously and place a knob of butter on top of each fish piece.
3. Mix coconut cream, curry paste, and chopped cilantro in a small bowl and pour over the fish. Bake in the oven for 20 minutes or until the fish is done.
4. In the meantime, cut the cauliflower into small florets and boil in lightly salted water for a couple of minutes. Serve with the fish.

Creamy Keto Fish Casserole

⏱ Cook Time:30 min		🍴 Serving:4					
🍤 Fat:15g		🥖 Carbogydrates:9g		🥩 Protein:27g		© Calories:221	

Ingredients

- 1 tbsp butter, for greasing baking dish
- 3 tbsp olive oil
- 1 lb broccoli, small florets
- 1 tsp salt
- ½ tsp ground black pepper
- 4 oz. (1¼ cups) scallions, finely chopped
- 2 tbsp small capers (non-pareils)
- 1½ lbs white fish (see tip), cut into serving-sized pieces
- 1 tbsp dried parsley
- 1¼ cups heavy whipping cream
- 1 tbsp Dijon mustard
- 3 oz. butter, cut into thin, equal slices

Instructions

1. Preheat oven to 400°F (200°C). Grease a 13" x 9" (33 x 23 cm) baking dish, set aside.
2. Heat the oil in a large frying pan, over medium-high heat. Add the broccoli, and stir-fry for 5 minutes, or until lightly browned and tender. Season with salt and pepper.
3. Add the scallions and capers, stir together, and fry for a couple of minutes. Spoon the broccoli mixture into the baking dish.
4. Place the fish amongst the vegetables.
5. In a medium-sized bowl, whisk together the parsley, whipping cream, and mustard. Pour over the fish and vegetables. Top with the sliced butter.
6. Bake on the middle rack, uncovered, for 20 minutes or until the fish is cooked through, and flakes easily with a fork.

55

7. Serve as is, or with leafy greens on the side.

Grilled Salmon with Avocado Salsa

⏱ Cook Time:22 min	🍴 Serving:2		

Carbohydrates:13g Protein:25g © Calories:528

Ingredients

- 1/4 teaspoon black pepper
- 1/4 teaspoon salt
- For the avocado salsa
- 1 ripe avocado pitted and diced
- 1/2 cup tomato diced (any type of tomato)
- 2 4-6 oz salmon fillets
- 2 tablespoons onion diced
- 2 tablespoons olive oil
- 2 tablespoons cilantro minced
- 1 clove garlic minced or crushed
- 1 tablespoon olive oil
- 1/2 teaspoon
- 1 tablespoon lime juice
- 1/2 teaspoon
- salt and pepper to taste
- 1/2 teaspoon onion powder

Instructions

1. Stir the olive oil, garlic, and spices in a small bowl. Brush or rub salmon with the spice mixture.

2. Heat a large heavy-duty (preferably non-stick) pan or grill medium-high heat. Add salmon to the pan and cook for 5-6 minutes per side. Remove from pan, top with avocado salsa and serve immediately.

3. To make the avocado salsa: Add the avocado, tomato, onion, and cilantro to a large mixing bowl. Drizzle with olive oil, fresh lime juice and a pinch of salt and pepper. Gently mix with a spoon until fully combined. Cover with plastic wrap until ready to serve.

(Instant Pot) Coconut Curry Mussels with Zucchini Noodles

⏱ Cook Time:25 min	🐾 Serving:4				
🍳 Fat:20g	🍰 Carbogydrates:11g	😊 Protein:10g	© Calories:269

Ingredients

- 4 cloves garlic, minced
- 1 tablespoon red curry paste
- 1 cup coconut milk
- 1 cup chicken broth
- ¾ pound (15 to 18) mussels, scrubbed, beards removed
- ½ medium red bell pepper, cut into strips
- tablespoons avocado oil
- 1 tablespoon fish sauce
- 1 (10- to 12-ounce) package zucchini noodles or 2 large zucchini, zoodled
- ½ teaspoon fine Himalayan pink salt
- ⅓ cup diced onion
- ¼ teaspoon black pepper
- 2 tablespoons minced fresh ginger
- Juice of ½ lime
- ¼ cup chopped fresh cilantro, for serving

Instructions

1. Select SAUTÉ on the Instant Pot. When the pot is hot, add 1 table- spoon of the avocado oil. Add the zucchini noodles to the hot oil and cook, stirring frequently, until just tender, 3 to 4 minutes. Select CANCEL. Transfer the zoodles to a dish and cover to keep warm.

2. Select SAUTÉ again. Add the remaining 2 tablespoons avocado oil to the pot. When the oil is hot, add the onion, ginger, garlic, and curry paste. Cook, stirring

frequently, until fragrant, about 1 minute. Select CANCEL. Add the coconut milk, broth, mussels, and bell pep-per to the pot.

3. Secure the lid and close the pressure-release valve. Set the pot to HIGH pressure for 3 minutes. At the end of the cooking time, quick- release the pressure. Discard any mussels that have not opened.

4. Divide the zucchini noodles and mussels among four shallow serving bowls. Stir the fish sauce, pink salt, pepper, and lime juice into the curry sauce, then pour over the mussels. Sprinkle with cilantro before serving

Poultry Dishes

Crispy Chipotle Chicken Thighs

⏱	Cook Time:30 min	🍢	Serving:3				
🍖	Fat:20g	🍰	Carbogydrates:33g	🥛	Protein:25g	©	Calories:400

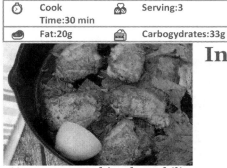

Ingredients

- ¼ teaspoon ground coriander
- ¼ teaspoon smoked paprika
- 12 ounces boneless chicken thighs
- ½teaspoon chipotle chili powder
- Salt and pepper
- 1 tablespoon olive oil
- ¼ teaspoon garlic powder
- ¼ teaspoon onion powder
- 3 cups fresh baby spinach

Instructions

1. Combine the chipotle chili powder, garlic powder, onion powder, coriander, and smoked paprika in a small bowl.

2. Pound the chicken thighs out flat, then season with salt and pepper on both sides.

3. Cut the chicken thighs in half and heat the oil in a heavy skillet over medium-high heat.

4. Add the chicken thighs skin-side-down to the skillet and sprinkle with the spice mixture.

5. Cook the chicken thighs for 8 minutes then flip and cook on the other side for 3 to 5 minutes.

6. During the last 3 minutes, add the spinach to the skillet and cook until wilted. Serve the crispy chicken thighs on a bed of wilted spinach.

Chicken Breast with Eggplant, Zucchini and Spinach

⏱	Cook Time:25 min	🍳	Serving:3				
🍢	Fat:20.4g	🍞	Carbogydrates:14g	☺	Protein:35g	©	Calories:369

Ingredients

- 150 g mushrooms, sliced
- 1 clove garlic, minced
- 1/3 medium onion chopped in small pieces or sliced
- 1 tbsp ghee

For the marinade (optional):

- 3 tbsp extra virgin olive oil
- 1/5 cup lemon juice
- 2 cloves garlic, minced
- 1/4 tsp salt
- 1 tsp black pepper

- 400 g chicken breast, skinless
- 1 medium zucchini diced, unpeeled
- ½ edium eggplant diced, unpeeled
- 2 cups spinach, cut in pieces

Instructions

1. If you like to marinate the chicken, combine the ingredients for the marinade together in a bowl. Stir well.
2. Dice the chicken. Place in a bag or plastic box along with the marinade. Leave in the fridge for 3 hours.
3. Heat a tablespoon of ghee in a large pan. Sauté the minced garlic and onion in the oil for 2-3 minutes. Stir occasionally.
4. Slice the eggplant into cubes and toss these into the pan. Cook for another 2-3 minutes.

5. Cut the mushroom into slices and then dice the zucchini. Add them into the pan as well. Leave to cook. This may take an additional 2-3 minutes.

6. Stir the chicken into the vegetable mixture for 6-7 minutes to cook thoroughly.

7. Put the spinach in and leave for 5 minutes more. When the leaves wilt, remove from the heat.

Serve in a bowl and enjoy.

Easy Cashew Chicken

⏱ Cook Time:10 min	🍴 Serving:3				
🥩 Fat:24g	🍞 Carbogydrates:8g	🥤 Protein:22g	© Calories:330		

Ingredients

- 1/2 medium green bell pepper
- 1/2 teaspoon ground ginger
- 1 tablespoon rice wine vinegar
- 1 1/2 tablespoons liquid aminos
- 1/2 tablespoon chili garlic sauce
- 1 tablespoon minced garlic
- 1 tablespoon sesame oil
- 1 tablespoon sesame seeds
- 1 tablespoon green onions
- 1/4 medium white onion
- Salt and pepper, to taste

- 3 raw chicken thighs, boneless and skinless
- 2 tablespoons coconut oil (for cooking)
- 1/4 cup raw cashews

Instructions

1. Heat a pan over low heat and toast the cashews for 8 minutes, or until they start to lightly brown and become fragrant. Remove and set aside.

2. Dice chicken thighs into 1 inch chunks. Cut onion and pepper into equally large chunks.

3. Increase heat to high and add coconut oil to pan.

4. Once oil is up to temperature, add in the chicken thighs and allow them to cook through (about 5 minutes).

5. Once the chicken is fully cooked add in the pepper, onions, garlic, chili garlic sauce, and seasonings (ginger, salt, pepper). Allow to cook on high for 2-3 minutes.

6. Add liquid aminos, rice wine vinegar, and cashews. Cook on high and allow the liquid to reduce down until it is a sticky consistency. There should not be excess liquid in the pan upon completing cooking.

7. Serve in a bowl, top with sesame seeds, and drizzle with sesame oil. Enjoy!

Thai Chicken Lettuce Wraps

⏱	Cook Time:10 min	🍴	Serving:4				
🍖	Fat:14g	🏠	Carbogydrates:8g	🔵 Protein:21g	©	Calories:270	

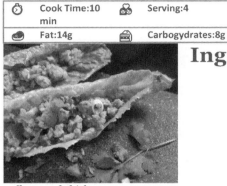

Ingredients

- 1 lb ground chicken
- 1 tablespoon olive oil
- 2 tablespoons red curry paste
- 1 tablespoon ginger, minced
- 4 cloves garlic, minced
- 1 red bell pepper, sliced thinly
- 4 green onions, chopped
- 1 cup cabbage, shredded or coleslaw mix
- 1/4 cup hoisin sauce
- 1/4 teaspoon salt, or to taste
- 1/4 teaspoon pepper, or to taste
- 5 leaves basil, chopped
- 1/2 head iceberg lettuce, cut into half

Instructions

1. Add olive oil to a large skillet and heat until oil is very hot. Add ground chicken and cook until no longer pink and starts to brown, break it up with a wooden spoon as necessary. Should take about 3 minutes.
2. Add red curry paste, ginger, garlic, peppers, coleslaw mix, and stir-fry for another 3 minutes. Add hoisin sauce and green onions, and toss. Remove from heat then add basil and toss. Transfer cooked chicken to a bowl.
3. Serve by placing spoonfuls of chicken into pieces of lettuce, fold lettuce over like small tacos, and eat.

64

Turkey Meatballs

⏱ Cook Time:25 min	🍴 Serving:6			
🍖 Fat:16g	🍞 Carbogydrates:4g	🍗 Protein:28g	©	Calories:234

Ingredients

- 2 lbs
ground turkey
- 3 tbsp tomato sauce
- 1/3 cup chopped yellow onion
- 1/2 tsp onion powder

- 1/2 tsp dried parsley
- 1 tsp oregano
- 1 tsp salt
- 1/4 tsp pepper (or more to taste)
- 1 1/2 tbsp olive oil
- 1 large egg
- 3/4 cup almond flour
- 1–2 cloves finely chopped garlic
- 1 tsp coconut aminos

Instructions

1. Preheat oven to 375 F. Coat a rimmed baking sheet with nonstick cooking spray.
2. In a large mixing bowl, add the ground turkey, almond flour, salt, garlic, onion powder, oregano, pepper, and parsley. Stir well to combine.
3. In a small bowl, beat the egg, then add it along with the coconut aminos, onions and tomato sauce to the meat mixture. Mix together with hands until evenly combined.
4. Using a spoon, scoop the meat and shape into 1 1/2-inch meatballs (size of a golf balls).
5. Transfer and arrange on the prepared baking sheet. You should have about 18-20 meatballs total.
6. Brush the tops of the meatballs with the olive oil.
7. Bake for 15-20 minutes, or until the internal temperature of the meatballs read 165 F on a meat thermometer.

8. Serve as an appetizer or add a veggie and turn this into a complete meal. I love adding this on top of salads for a great meal-prep lunch option.

Roasted Turkey Breast with Mushrooms & Brussels Sprouts

⏱ Cook Time:50 min		🍳 Serving:4			
🍲 Fat:9g		🍱 Carbogydrates:6g	🍲 Protein:27g	©	Calories:210

Ingredients

- 1 tsp garlic powder
- 1 pound turkey breast raw, cut into 1 inch cubes
- 1/2 pound brussels sprouts cleaned, cut in half
- 1 cups mushrooms cleaned

- 2 tbsp olive oil
- 1 tsp salt
- 1 tsp black pepper

Instructions

1. Preheat oven to 350 degrees Fahrenheit.

2. In a small mixing bowl, combine olive oil, salt, black pepper, and garlic powder.

3. In a 9 x 6-inch casserole dish, combine turkey, brussels sprouts, and mushrooms. Pour the olive oil mixture over the top.

4. Cover with foil and bake for 45 minutes or until the turkey is cooked through and no longer pink. An internal temperature of 165 degrees Fahrenheit is a safe bet.

Turkey and Bacon Lettuce Wraps

⏱	Cook Time:15 min	🍴	Serving:4				
🍳	Fat:20g	🍞	Carbogydrates:22g	☺	Protein:11g	©	Calories:305

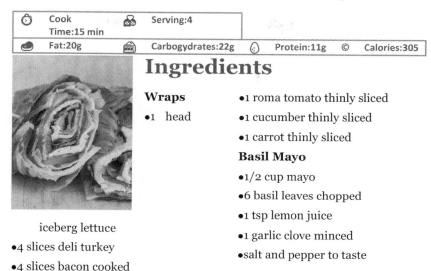

Ingredients

Wraps

• 1   head

iceberg lettuce

• 4 slices deli turkey

• 4 slices bacon cooked

• 1 avocado thinly sliced

• 1 roma tomato thinly sliced

• 1 cucumber thinly sliced

• 1 carrot thinly sliced

Basil Mayo

• 1/2 cup mayo

• 6 basil leaves chopped

• 1 tsp lemon juice

• 1 garlic clove minced

• salt and pepper to taste

Instructions

Basil Mayo

1. Combine all of the ingredients in a food processor, blend until smooth

Wraps

1. Lay out two large lettuce leaves then layer on 1 slice of turkey and slather with Basil-Mayo.

2. Layer on a second slice of turkey followed by the bacon, and a few slices of avocado, tomato, cucumber and carrot.

3. Season lightly with salt and pepper then fold the bottom up, the sides in, and roll like a burrito.

4. Slice in half and serve cold.

Chiken Stir-Fry

⏱	Cook Time:40 min	⚙	Serving:4				
🍳	Fat:14g	🏠	Carbogydrates:11g	💧 Protein:31g	©	Calories:312	

Ingredients

●3

boneless, skinless chicken breasts, trimmed and cut into pieces at least 1 inch square

●2 red bell peppers

●2 cups sugar snap peas

●1 1/2 T peanut oil

●1-2 T sesame seeds, preferably black

Marinade ingredients:

●1/3 cup soy sauce (gluten-free if needed)

●2 T unseasoned (unsweetened) rice vinegar

●2 T low-carb sweetener of your choice (see notes)

●1 T sesame oil

●1/2 tsp. garlic powder

Instructions

1. Trim the chicken breasts and cut into pieces at least 1 inch square.

2. Combine soy sauce, rice vinegar, Stevia, agave or maple syrup, sesame oil and garlic powder.

3. Put the chicken into a Ziploc bag and pour in HALF the marinade. Let chicken marinate in the fridge for at least 4 hours (or all day while you're at work would be even better.)

4. When you're ready to cook, cover a large baking sheet with foil, then put it in the oven and let the pan get hot while the oven heats to 425F/220C.

68

5. Drain the marinated chicken well in a colander placed in the sink.

6. Remove the hot baking sheet from the oven and spread the chicken out over the surface (so pieces are not touching). Put baking sheet into the oven and cook chicken 8 minutes.

7. While the chicken cooks, trim ends of the sugar snap peas. Cut out the core and seeds of the red bell peppers and discard; then cut peppers into strips about the same thickness as the sugar snap peas.

8. Put veggies into a bowl and toss with the peanut oil.

9. After 8 minutes, remove pan from the oven and arrange the veggies around the chicken, trying to have each vegetable piece touching the pan as much as you can.

10. Put back into the oven and cook about 12 minutes more, or until the chicken is cooked through and lightly browned.

11. Brush cooked chicken and vegetables with the remaining marinade and sprinkle with black sesame seeds. Serve hot.

Keto Smothered Chicken Thighs

⏱ Cook Time:1 hours	🍴 Serving:4				
🍖 Fat:32g	🍞 Carbogydrates:2.5g	🥛 Protein:40g	© Calories:466		

Ingredients

•4

(8 ounce) skin-on, bone-in chicken thighs

•1 teaspoon paprika

•salt and pepper to taste

•4 slices bacon, cut into 1/2 inch pieces

•⅓ cup low-sodium chicken broth

•4 ounces sliced mushrooms

•¼ cup heavy whipping cream

•2 green onions, white and green parts separated and sliced

Instructions

1. Preheat the oven to 400 degrees F (200 degrees C).

2. Season chicken thighs on all sides with paprika, salt, and pepper.

3. Cook bacon in a cast iron skillet or oven-safe pan over medium-high heat until browned, 4 to 5 minutes. Remove from skillet and drain on a paper towel-lined plate. Drain and discard excess grease from skillet.

4. Return skillet to medium heat and cook chicken thighs, skin-side down, for 3 to 4 minutes. Flip chicken over and place skillet in the preheated oven.

5. Bake until chicken thighs are no longer pink at the bone and juices run clear, about 30 minutes. An instant-read thermometer inserted near the bone

70

should read 165 degrees F (74 degrees C). Remove chicken to a plate and cover with foil to keep warm. Remove all but 2 tablespoons drippings from skillet.

6. Return skillet to the stove over medium-high heat. Pour in chicken broth while whisking up brown bits from the bottom of the skillet. Add mushrooms and cook until soft, about 3 to 4 minutes. Pour in heavy whipping cream and whisk together until lightly simmering, then reduce heat to medium-low. Season with salt and pepper, if necessary.

7. Return chicken and any juices back into skillet; top with bacon and green onions. Serve immediately, spooning sauce over the chicken.

Keto Chiken Curry

⏱ Cook Time:30 min	👪 Serving:2				
🍤 Fat:17g	🥫 Carbogydrates:8g	🥄 Protein:14g	© Calories:250

Ingredients

- 0.67 tbsp Olive oil (divided)
- 0.17 large Onion (chopped)
- 0.33 lb Chicken breast (cut into bite size pieces)
- 0.33 14.5-oz can Diced tomatoes (drained)
- 2.33 oz Coconut cream (the entire cream part skimmed from a 14-oz can)
- 0.08 cup Chicken broth
- 1.33 cloves Garlic (minced)
- 0.5 tbsp Curry powder (+1 tsp cumin if your curry powder doesn't include it)
- 0.33 tsp Ground ginger
- 0.33 tsp Paprika
- 0.17 tsp Sea salt (to taste)

Instructions

1. Heat oil in a large saute pan over medium heat. Add the onion and saute for about 7 to 10 minutes, until translucent and browned.
2. Push the onion to the side. Increase heat to medium high. Add another tablespoon oil and the chicken in a single layer. Saute the chicken for just 1 to 2 minutes per side, only to brown the outside.
3. Add the diced tomatoes, coconut cream, chicken broth, garlic, curry powder, ground ginger, paprika, and sea salt. Stir everything together. Adjust salt to taste.
4. Bring the mixture to a boil, then reduce heat, cover, and simmer for about 15 to 20 minutes, until the

chicken is cooked through, sauce is thick, and flavors develop to your liking.

Keto Fried Chicken

⏱ Cook Time:20 min	🍳 Serving:3				
🍢 Fat:12.5g	📦 Carbogydrates:1g	🥄 Protein:6g	© Calories:140		

Ingredients

- 1 cup coconut oil
- 6 chicken thighs boneless skinless, about 1.5 lbs/6 thighs, patted dry with paper towels
- 2 eggs
- 1 teaspoon black pepper divided
- 1 1/2 teaspoons salt
- 3.5 oz. bag pork rinds crushed in the bag or in food processor
- 1/2 cup grated Parmesan
- 2 teaspoons paprika
- 1 teaspoon cayenne pepper

Instructions

1. Heat your oven to 350°F.
2. In a shallow bowl, whisk the eggs and 1/3 teaspoon black pepper together.
3. In another shallow bowl, mix together the remaining black pepper, salt, crushed pork rinds, Parmesan cheese, paprika, and cayenne.
4. One at a time, dip your chicken thighs into the egg mixture and then dredge in the pork rind mixture to fully coat. Make sure to press the crumbs into the surface and crevices of the chicken firmly.
5. Heat the coconut oil in a cast-iron skillet over high heat. Once the oil begins to smoke, place in the chicken thighs in the skillet.
6. Fry the chicken thighs for 2-3 minutes on one side and then flip and fry for another 2-3 minutes until the crust is golden brown.

7. Transfer the chicken thighs to the baking sheet and bake for an additional 10-15 minutes, until the internal temperature reaches 170-175°F.

Grilled Chicken with Avocado Salsa

⏱	Cook Time:25 min	🐾	Serving:4				
🍲	Fat:30g	🍞	Carbogydrates:12g	☻	Protein:40g	©	Calories:470

Ingredients

•1

- •½ tsp paprika
- •½ tsp salt or to taste
- •¼ tsp black pepper

Avocado Salsa

- •2 avocados diced
- •2 small (or 1 large tomato) chopped
- •¼ cup red onion chopped
- •1 jalapeno de-seeded and chopped (optional)
- •1/4 cup cilantro finely chopped
- •Juice of 1 lime
- •fresh cracked pepper & salt to taste

1/2 pounds boneless skinless chicken breasts or 4 chicken breasts

- •2 garlic cloves finely minced
- •3 tablespoons olive oil
- •¼ cup cilantro chopped
- •Juice of 1 lime
- •1/2 tsp. cumin

Instructions

1. In a large bowl, whisk all the ingredients for the marinade and set aside.

2. Pound the breasts to even thickness or slice in half horizontally to get evenly sized breasts and add to the bowl of marinade. Mix through until the chicken is fully coated in the marinade. Use right away if needed or marinate for 30-minutes or up to 12 hours.

3. Grill chicken over medium-high heat or in a large on the stovetop for 5-6 minutes per side or until the inside is cooked through and the outside is charred. Top with fresh avocado salsa and serve immediately.

75

To Make Avocado Salsa

1. While the chicken is grilled, combine all the ingredients for the salsa in a small bowl. Cover with plastic wrap in the fridge until ready to use.

Rosemary Chicken Salad with Avocado and Bacon

⏱ Cook Time:30 min	🍴 Serving:2				
🍲 Fat:25g	🍞 Carbogydrates:12g	🥗 Protein:29g	© Calories:380		

Ingredients

- 3 slices center-cut bacon, diced
- 2 boneless, trimmed skinless chicken thighs (4 oz each)
- 1/2 teaspoon kosher salt
- 1 tbsp fresh rosemary
- 3 cups chopped romaine lettuce, chopped
- 1/2 cup baby arugula or watercress
- 1/2 cup halved cherry tomatoes
- 3 tablespoons chopped red onion
- 4 oz avocado, sliced (1 small)

For the rosemary vinaigrette:

- 1 tsp dijon mustard
- 4 tsp olive oil
- 2 tbsp red wine vinegar
- 1/2 tsp fresh minced rosemary
- 1/4 teaspoon kosher salt

Instructions

76

1. Cook bacon in a large heavy nonstick skillet until crispy, about 7 minutes. Transfer to a paper towel to drain and set aside.

2. Drain the fat but don't wipe the skillet, leaving any excess oil in the pan to cook the chicken.

3. Season chicken with salt and rosemary, cook in the skillet over medium-high heat until golden and cooked through, about 5 minutes on each side.

4. Make a bed of the romaine and arugula (or watercress) in a large serving bowl or platter (or divide between 2 plates). Scatter the cherry tomatoes, red onion and bacon on top.

5. Slice the avocado, sprinkle with pinch of salt and arrange on salad. Slice the chicken thighs and add to the salad.

6. To make the rosemary vinaigrette, in a small bowl whisk the ingredients. Pour over the salad and serve right away.

Garlic, Lemon & Thyme Roasted Chicken Breasts

⏱ Cook Time: 2 hours 45 minutes	🍳 Serving:4		
🍖 Fat:12g	🍰 Carbogydrates:4g	☺ Protein:26g	© Calories:230

Ingredients

- juice of 1 lemon
- 1/2 cup extra virgin olive oil
- 4 cloves garlic minced
- 1 tablespoon fresh thyme
- 1 teaspoon salt
- 1/2 teaspoon ground black pepper
- 1 tablespoon olive oil for sauteing
- 4 boneless skinless chicken breasts
- zest of 1 lemon

Instructions

1. Create the marinade by mixing the lemon juice, zest, 1/2 cup of olive oil, garlic, thyme, salt, and pepper. Place the chicken breasts in a non-reactive glass dish, or plastic ziptop bag, and pour the marinade over the chicken. Make sure to evenly coat the chicken, then cover and refrigerate for 2 hours.

2. Preheat your oven to 400 degrees F. Remove the chicken from the marinade and wipe off the excess. Heat 1 tablespoon of olive oil, and sear the chicken breasts for 2 minutes on each side, until they're golden brown.

3. Place the chicken breasts on a baking sheet lined with a baking rack, and roast at 400 degrees F for 20-30 minutes

depending on the thickness of the chicken breast, or until the internal temperature reads 165 degrees F.

Grilled Chicken Kabobs

⏱	Cook Time: 30 minutes	🍴	Serving:2				
🍲	Fat 12g	🎂	Carbogydrates:26g	🥄	Protein:27g	©	Calories:278

Ingredients

- 0.5 pound boneless skinless chicken breasts cut into 1 inch pieces
- 0.13 cup olive oil
- 0.17 cup soy sauce
- 0.13 cup honey
- 0.5 teaspoon minced garlic
- salt and pepper to taste
- 0.5 red bell pepper cut into 1 inch pieces
- 0.5 yellow bell pepper cut into 1 inch pieces
- 1 small zucchini cut into 1 inch slices
- 0.5 red onion cut into 1 inch pieces
- 0.5 tablespoon chopped parsley

Instructions

1. Place the olive oil, soy sauce, honey, garlic and salt and pepper in a large bowl.
2. Whisk to combine.
3. Add the chicken, bell peppers, zucchini and red onion to the bowl. Toss to coat in the marinade.
4. Cover and refrigerate for at least 1 hour, or up to 8 hours.
5. Soak wooden skewers in cold water for at least 30 minutes. Preheat grill or grill pan to medium high heat.
6. Thread the chicken and vegetables onto the skewers.

79

7. Cook for 5-7 minutes on each side or until chicken is cooked through.
8. Sprinkle with parsley and serve.

Pork

Basil Tomato Pork Chops

⏱	Cook Time: 1 hr 20 min	🐾	Serving:4				
🍖	Fat 10g	🍰	Carbogydrates:9g	☺	Protein:21g	©	Calories:210

Ingredients

- 2 tablespoons olive oil
- 1 teaspoon finely chopped fresh garlic
- 8 (1/2-inch thick) pork chops
- 1 (28-ounce) can whole tomatoes, undrained, cut up
- 1 teaspoon dried basil leaves
- 1 teaspoon salt
- 1/2 teaspoon pepper
- 1/2 cup water
- 3 tablespoons cornstarch
- 1 medium green bell pepper, cut into rings
- 1 medium onion, cut into rings

Instructions

1. Melt butter in 12-inch skillet until sizzling; stir in garlic. Add 4 pork chops. Cook over medium-high heat, turning occasionally,4-6 minutes or until browned on both sides. Remove from pan; set aside. Repeat with remaining pork chops.

2. Return pork chops to pan. Stir in tomatoes, basil, salt and pepper. Cook over medium-high heat 3-4 minutes or until mixture comes to a boil. Reduce heat to low. Cover; cook, stirring occasionally, 50-60 minutes or until pork chops are no longer pink. Remove pork chops; keep warm.

3. Stir together water and cornstarch in small bowl. Stir cornstarch mixture into hot cooking liquid with wire whisk; add green pepper and onion.

4. Increase heat to medium-high. Cook, stirring occasionally, 5-6 minutes or until mixture is thickened and vegetables are crisply tender. Serve sauce over pork chops

Slow-Roasted Pork with Citrus and Garlic

⏱	Cook Time: 2 hr 30 min	🐾	Serving:8				
🍲	Fat 16g	🍞	Carbogydrates:9g	☺	Protein:21g	©	Calories:420

Ingredients

- 10 cloves garlic
- 2 tablespoons fresh oregano
- 1 tablespoon fresh thyme
- 2 tablespoons coriander seeds
- 2 teaspoons cumin seeds
- 4 bay leaves
- Kosher salt and freshly ground pepper
- 1 6-to-8-pound Boston butt pork shoulder
- Juice of 6 oranges, peels reserved
- Juice of 4 lemons, peels reserved
- Juice of 4 limes
- 1/4 cup Worcestershire sauce
- 3/4 cup extra-virgin olive oil
- 3 white onions, thinly sliced

Instructions

1. Pulse the garlic, oregano, thyme, coriander and cumin seeds, bay leaves, 2 tablespoons salt and 1 teaspoon pepper in a food processor to make a thick paste. Trim off all but a thin layer of fat from the pork, then make deep slits all over the roast (about every 2 inches) with a paring knife. Rub the spice paste over the pork and into the slits.

83

2. Mix the citrus juices, Worcestershire sauce and olive oil in a large glass bowl. Submerge the pork in the marinade and top with the onions and reserved orange and lemon peels. Cover with plastic wrap and refrigerate at least 8 hours or up to 2 days. Bring to room temperature 1 hour before roasting.

3. Preheat the oven to 450. Remove the citrus peels from the bowl and refrigerate. Place the pork on a rack in a large roasting pan (reserve the marinade and onions); roast, uncovered, about 1 hour. Add the marinade to the pan and pile the onions on top of the meat. Cover with foil, lower the oven temperature to 350 and roast 2 more hours. Uncover, place the citrus peels around the pork and continue to roast, basting occasionally, until the meat browns and a thermometer inserted into the bottom half registers 190, 1 hour 30 minutes to 2 hours.

4. Transfer the pork to a cutting board and let rest 10 minutes. Meanwhile, skim any excess fat from the pan juices. Slice the pork and serve with the onion and pan juices. Garnish with citrus peels.

The Best Baked Garlic Pork Tenderloin

⏱ Cook Time: 1 hour	🐾 Serving:4				
🍖 Fat 13g	🍰 Carbogydrates:6g	🥤 Protein:32g	© Calories:449		

Ingredients

- 2 tbsp extra virgin olive oil
- 1 tbsp celtic sea salt and fresh cracked pepper
- 2 lb pork tenderloin, optional: pre-marinate pork before cooking
- 4 tbsp butter, sliced into 4-6 pats
- 2 tbsp diced garlic
- 1 tsp dried basil*
- 1 tsp dried oregano*
- 1 tsp dried thyme*
- 1 tsp dried parsley*
- ½ tsp dried sage*
- 2 tbsp Italian Herb Seasoning Blend

Instructions

5. Preheat oven to 350 degrees.
6. Line baking sheet with aluminum foil.
7. In a small bowl, combine garlic, basil, oregano, thyme, parsley, and sage. Set aside.
8. Generously season meat with salt and pepper.
9. In a large pan, heat oil until shimmery.
10. Add to pan, and cook on all sides until dark golden brown.
11. Transfer to baking sheet.
12. Generously coat with herb mix.
13. Place pats of butter on top of the pork.

85

14. Wrap in foil, bake until meat is 150 degrees internally at the widest, thickest part of the tenderloin (about 25 minutes.)

15. When pork has come to temperature, remove and let rest, tented with foil, for at least five minutes to lock in juices.

16. Slice against the grain and serve immediately.

17. To store leftovers, place in an airtight container and keep in refrigerator for up to three days.

18. To freeze leftovers, place in a plastic bag or wrap in plastic wrap and keep in freezer for up to three months.

19. To reheat, let thaw naturally in the refrigerator overnight, and bake at 350, wrapped in foil, until piping hot when ready to serve.

Coffee-Chipotle Pork Chops

⏱	Cook Time:35 min	🐄	Serving:4				
🍖	Fat 10g	🍞	Carbogydrates:6g	🥤	Protein:15g	©	Calories:200

Ingredients

- 4 (4 ounce) boneless pork loin chops
- ⅓ teaspoon salt
- ⅓ teaspoon ground black pepper
- 1 teaspoons and ⅓ teaspoon olive oil, divided
- shallots, minced
- 1 teaspoons and ⅓ teaspoon dried thyme leaves
- ½ cup sweet port wine
- ½ cup blackberry juice
- ½ cup chicken broth
- 2 teaspoons balsamic vinegar
- 1 teaspoons and ⅓ teaspoon cornstarch
- 1 teaspoons and ⅓ teaspoon water
- 2 tablespoons and 2 teaspoons fresh blackberries

Instructions

1. Mix all of the ingredients for the rub in a small bowl. Rinse and pat dry pork chops and score the fat cap of the pork chops at 1 inch intervals. Then thoroughly rub both sides of the pork chops with the spice mixture until well coated, and reserve any remaining spice rub for another use (there will verily likely be some left over). Place rubbed pork chops in a large bag or container, and let sit in the fridge for at least 8 hours but preferably overnight.
2. Once the pork chops have sat in the fridge pull them out 30 minutes prior to cooking to allow to come to

87

room temperature. Preheat the oven to 350 degrees fahrenheit. In a large oven safe pan or skillet heat cooking fat of choice over medium high heat until very hot and then add pork chops while avoiding overcrowding the pan and sear 2-3 minutes each side.

3. Place pan or skillet in the oven for 10 minutes or until pork reaches 145 degrees. Remove from the oven and place pork chops on a cutting board and allow to rest for at least 10 minutes.

Coconut Pork Curry

⏱ Cook Time:60 min	🏋 Serving:4				
🥩 Fat 16g	🍱 Carbogydrates:10g	⚗ Protein:18g	©	Calories:260

Ingredients

- 1 teaspoon ground cumin
- 1 teaspoon ground coriander
- 1/2 teaspoon ground cinnamon
- 1/4 teaspoon ground chilli powder
- 800g diced pork
- 1 tablespoon vegetable oil

- 1 large (200g) brown onion, chopped
- 2 cloves garlic, chopped
- 4cm piece (20g) fresh ginger, grated
- 1 tablespoon water
- 400ml can coconut cream or coconut milk
- 2 tablespoons brown sugar
- 1 teaspoon salt
- 1 tablespoon lemon juice
- 1/4 cup fresh coriander leaves

Instructions

1. Combine the spices in a medium bowl; add pork, toss to coat.

2. Heat half the oil in a large frying pan. Cook the pork in 2 batches, using the remaining oil, until browned all over. Remove from pan.

3. Add onion to same pan with garlic, ginger and water; cook, stirring, over medium heat until

89

softened. Return the pork to the pan with coconut cream, sugar and salt. Simmer, covered, stirring occasionally, for about 1 hour to 1 hour 30 minutes or until the pork is tender and the sauce is thickened.

4. Stir in juice; season to taste with salt and pepper. Sprinkle with coriander.

Pan-Seared Pork Tenderloin Medallions

⏱ Cook Time:18 min	🍽 Serving:4		
🥩 Fat 7g	🍰 Carbogydrates:3g	☺ Protein:18g	© Calories:150

Ingredients

- 1 tablespoon canola oil 1 (1-lb.)
- pork tenderloin, trimmed and cut crosswise into 12 medallions
- 1/2 teaspoon kosher salt
- 1/4 teaspoon garlic powder
- 1/4 teaspoon black pepper Fresh thyme leaves (optional)

Instructions

1. Heat oil in a 12-inch skillet over medium-high. Arrange pork medallions in a single layer on a work surface, and press each with the palm of your hand to flatten to an even thickness.

2. Combine salt, garlic powder, and pepper; sprinkle evenly over pork. Add pork to skillet in a single layer; cook just until done, about 3 minutes per side

3. Remove from heat; let stand 5 minutes before serving. Garnish with thyme leaves, if desired.

Pork Rind Pork Chops

⏱ Cook Time:20 min	🐖 Serving:4				
🥩 Fat 10g	🍰 Carbogydrates:3g	💧 Protein:51g	©	Calories:495

Ingredients

- 2 oz pork rinds
- 8 thin cut boneless pork chops, ½-inch thick
- 2 tablespoons Dijon mustard
- ½ teaspoon Diamond Crystal kosher salt
- ½ teaspoon black pepper
- ½ teaspoon garlic powder
- Olive oil spray

Instructions

1. Place the pork rinds in a 1-gallon ziploc bag. Use a meat pounder or a rolling pin to crush them into small crumbs, similar to Panko. You can also crush the pork rinds in a food processor. Set the crushed pork rinds aside.
2. Use a pastry brush (or your hands) to coat both sides of the pork chops with mustard. Sprinkle with salt, pepper, and garlic powder.
3. Place about 2 heaping tablespoons of the crushed pork rinds on a plate. Dip one pork chop into the pork rinds and press to coat on both sides. Repeat with the remaining pork chops.
4. Heat a double burner griddle over medium-high heat. Spray well with olive oil spray. Or brush the pan with 1-2 tablespoons olive oil.
5. Cook the pork chops until golden-brown and cooked through, about 5 minutes on each side. If the pan overheats,

lower the heat to medium. Serve the pork rind pork chops
immediately.

Pork Skewers with Chimichurri

⏱ Cook Time:20 min	🍴 Serving:2			
🍳 Fat 36g	🍲 Carbogydrates:3g	💧 Protein:30g	© Calories:450

Ingredients

- 1/2 pound boneless pork shoulder
- 1/4 teaspoon ground cumin
- 1/4 teaspoon paprika
- 1 tablespoon coconut oil
- 1/4 cup olive oil
- 1/4 cup diced green peppers
- 3 tablespoons fresh chopped parsley
- 1 tablespoon fresh chopped cilantro
- 1 1/2 tablespoons fresh lemon juice
- 1 garlic clove (minced)
- salt and pepper

Instructions

1. Cut the pork into slices about 1-inch thick.
2. Season the pork with salt, pepper, cumin and paprika.
3. Slide the pork slices onto wooden skewers and heat the coconut oil in a skillet.
4. Fry the skewers until both sides are browned and the meat is cooked through.
5. Combine the remaining ingredients in a food processor.
6. Pulse several times to chop then blend until smooth.
7. Serve the pork skewers with the chimichurri spooned over them.

Pork Meatballs

⏱ Cook Time:25 min	🐑 Serving:8		
🍖 Fat 24g	🍰 Carbogydrates:2g	😊 Protein:19g	© Calories:298

Ingredients

- 2 lb. ground pork
- 2 teaspoons Diamond Crystal kosher salt (not fine salt)
- ½ teaspoon black pepper
- 2 teaspoons onion powder
- 2 teaspoons garlic powder
- 2 teaspoons sweet paprika
- 1 teaspoons dried thyme
- 1 teaspoon coriander
- 1 teaspoon ground cumin

Instructions

1. Preheat your oven to 400 degrees F. Line a large rimmed baking sheet with parchment paper.

2. In a large bowl, use your clean hands to mix together all the ingredients.

3. Shape the mixture into 32 meatballs, each weighing about 1 oz (30 grams). It's easier to shape the meatballs if your hands are wet.

4. Arrange the meatballs in a single layer on the prepared baking sheet.

5. Bake them until browned and cooked through, about 15 minutes.

Pork Lettuce Wraps

⏲	Cook Time:15 min	🍢	Serving:4			
🫘	Fat 49g	🧈	Carbogydrates:12g	Protein:42g	©	Calories:660

Ingredients

- 1/2 pound boneless pork shoulder
- 1/4 teaspoon ground cumin
- 1/4 teaspoon paprika
- 1 tablespoon coconut oil
- 1/4 cup olive oil
- 1/4 cup diced green peppers
- 3 tablespoons fresh chopped parsley
- 1 tablespoon fresh chopped cilantro
- 1 1/2 tablespoons fresh lemon juice
- 1 garlic clove (minced)
- salt and pepper

Instructions

1. Cut the pork into slices about 1-inch thick.
2. Season the pork with salt, pepper, cumin and paprika.
3. Slide the pork slices onto wooden skewers and heat the coconut oil in a skillet.
4. Fry the skewers until both sides are browned and the meat is cooked through.
5. Combine the remaining ingredients in a food processor.
6. Pulse several times to chop then blend until smooth.
7. Serve the pork skewers with the chimichurri spooned over them.

Cajun Pork Tenderloin

⏱	Cook Time:25 min	🍴	Serving:4				
🥩	Fat 20g	🍰	Carbogydrates:2g	☺	Protein:51g	©	Calories:403

Ingredients

- 2 tablespoons Cajun Spice Blend (see below)
- 2 tablespoons Dijon mustard
- 2 tablespoons ghee
- 2 pork tenderloins (1 1/2 to 2 pounds total)
- Coarse sea salt, for garnish

Instructions

1. Preheat the oven to 375°F.
2. In a small mixing bowl, combine the spice blend, mustard, and ghee. Brush the mixture evenly onto the pork tenderloins.
3. Place a large cast-iron or other oven-safe skillet on the stovetop over medium-high heat.
4. When the pan is hot, sear the tenderloins on both sides until lightly browned, about 2 minutes per side.
5. Transfer the pan to the oven and roast the tenderloins for 15 to 20 minutes, until the internal temperature of the pork reaches at least 145°F. Garnish with coarse sea salt before serving.

Beef and Lamb

Keto Fajitas with Chicken and Beef

⏱	Cook Time:30 min	👥	Serving:6					
🥩	Fat 26g	🧀	Carbogydrates:6g	🍳	Protein:52g	©	Calories:450

Ingredients

- •2 teaspoons Chili Powder
- •2 teaspoons Kosher salt
- •1 teaspoon Smoked Paprika
- •1/2 teaspoon Onion powder
- •1/2 teaspoon Cumin
- •2 Tablespoons Avocado Oil
- •2 Boneless Skinless Chicken Breasts
- •1 pound Flank steak
- •1 Yellow bell pepper, sliced thin
- •1 Red Bell pepper, sliced thin
- •1 Medium White onion, sliced thin

Instructions

97

1. In a small mixing bowl combine chili powder, salt, paprika, onion powder, garlic powder and cumin.

2. Lay the chicken breast on a large cutting board and cut them in half lengthwise. This will help with even and faster cooking.

3. Sprinkle the seasoning generously over your chicken breast and steak. You will have some seasoning leftover...keep this to season your onions and bell peppers.

4. Add the avocado oil to a large skillet over medium high heat and sear your chicken until cooked through, cooking for a few minutes on each side until an internal thermometer reads 165F. Remove from the pan and set aside. Continue to cook the flank steak in the same skillet. Sear on each side until the internal temperature reaches your desired doneness. Medium is 145F. Let the steak rest while the onions and peppers are cooking.

5. Take your sliced onions and bell peppers and place them in your skillet. With your left-over fajita seasoning, sprinkle over veggies. Cook until tender.

6. Slice the chicken and beef for fajitas. Make sure when slicing your beef to slice against the grain to have super tender slices. Set aside.

7. Turn off heat and layer your perfectly seared chicken and beef steak on top of the onions and peppers. Serve with guacamole.

Keto Asian Steak Salad

⏱	Cook Time:15 min	🎎	Serving:2				
🍖	Fat 52g	🥞	Carbogydrates:4g	😊	Protein:31g	©	Calories:600

Ingredients

- •2 Ribeye Steaks
- •1/2 cup Soy sauce or coconut aminos divided
- •For the asian sesame dressing
- •1/2 cup Olive oil
- •2 tbsp Soy sauce or coconut aminos
- •2 tbsp Apple Cider Vinegar
- •1 tsp Sesame Oil
- •1/8 tsp liquid stevia
- •For assembling
- •4 cups Raw spinach
- •4 radishes sliced thin
- •Sesame seeds for garnish

Instructions

1. Place each steak in a zip top bag with 1/4 cup of soy sauce. Zip up the bags and allow to marinate on the counter for 1 hour.

99

2. Remove the steaks from the bag and discard the marinade. In a cast iron skillet on high heat, cook the steaks to your desired doneness. I did 4 minutes on each side for medium.

3. Let the steaks rest for 10 minutes on a cutting board.

4. While the steaks are resting, make your dressing. Add all of the dressing ingredients to a jar with a lid and shake to combine.

5. Assemble the salads. Add 2 cups of spinach and half of the sliced radish to each of the 2 bowls. Slice the steaks into 1/2 in thick pieces and add those to the salads. Drizzle the dressing on top and garnish with sesame seeds.

Easy Low Carb and Keto Chili without Beans

⏱	Cook Time: 1 hr 15 minutes	👥	Serving:8				
🍖	Fat 8g	🎂	Carbogydrates:10g	😋	Protein:22g	©	Calories:329

Ingredients

- 1 tbsp avocado oil (Click here for my favorite brand on Amazon)
- 1 lb Beef stew meat, Cut into bite size pieces
- 1 lb Ground Beef Chuck
- 1/2 Onion diced
- 1 Red Bell pepper diced
- 6 Cloves garlic minced
- 2 Tablespoons tomato paste
- 2 Tablespoons chili powder
- 1 Tablespoons garlic powder
- 1 Tablespoons onion powder
- 1 Tablespoons cumin
- 2 Tablespoons smoked paprika
- 1 28oz can Fire roasted diced tomatoes
- kosher salt to taste

Instructions

1. Heat a heavy pot over medium-high heat. Add the oil and the stew meat. Sauté until browned on all side. Remove stew meat from pot.

2. Add the onion, red bell pepper, and garlic to the pot. Saute' until translucent

3. Add the ground beef to the pot and saute' until cooked through. Add the tomato paste and the spices and stir to combine.

4. Add the sautéed stew meat, and crushed tomatoes, stir.

5. Place a lid on top, reduce the heat to low, and let simmer for 1 hours...or until the stew meat is tender.

6. Serve the chili with shredded cheese, cilantro, sour cream, and keto cornbread!

Keto Beef and Broccoli

⏱	Cook Time: 35 min	🍳	Serving:4				
🥩	Fat 14g	🍰	Carbogydrates:13g	☺	Protein:29g	©	Calories:294

Ingredients

- 1 pound flank steak sliced into 1/4 inch thick strips
- 5 cups small broccoli florets about 7 ounces
- 1 tablespoon avocado oil

For the sauce:

- 1 yellow onion sliced
- 1 Tbs butter
- ½ tbs olive oil
- 1/3 cup low-sodium soy sauce
- ⅓ cup beef stock
- 1 tablespoon fresh ginger minced
- 2 cloves garlic minced

Instructions

7. Heat avocado oil in a pan over medium heat for a few minutes or until hot.

8. Add sliced beef and cook until it browns, less than 5 minutes, don't stir too much, you want it to brown. Transfer to a plate and set aside.

9. Add onions to a skillet with butter and olive oil and cook 20 minutes until onions are caramelized and tender.

103

10. Add all other sauce ingredients into the skillet and stir the ingredients together over medium-low heat until it starts to simmer, about 5 minutes.

11. Use an immersion blender to blend sauce.

12. Keep the sauce warm over low heat, and add broccoli to the skillet.

13. Return beef to the pan and toss with broccoli and sauce top. Stir until everything is coated with the sauce.

14. Bring to a simmer and cook for another few minutes until broccoli is tender.

15. Season with salt and pepper to taste, if needed.

16. Serve immediately, optionally pairing with cooked cauliflower rice.

Keto Mongolian Beef

⏱	Cook Time: 25 min	⚖	Serving:4				
🍖	Fat 14g	🍰	Carbogydrates:17g	🥚	Protein:40g	©	Calories:35

Ingredients

- 1 Tablespoon avocado oil
- 2 teaspoons Minced ginger
- 1 Tablespoon Minced garlic
- 1/2 Cup Soy sauce or Coconut aminos
- 1/2 cup Water
- 3/4 cup Granulated sweetener
- 1 1/2 pounds Flank steak or Flatiron steak
- 1/4 teaspoon Red pepper flakes
- 5 Stems Green onions-cut diagonal into 2 inch pieces
- 1/4 teaspoon xanthan gum

Instructions

Making the sauce:

1. Heat 1 tablespoon Avocado Oil in a medium saucepan over medium heat.

2. Add ginger, garlic, red pepper flakes and stir for 30 seconds.

3. Add soy sauce, water and sweetener. Bring to a boil and simmer until thickened. Should take about 5 minutes.

4. Remove from skillet to a bowl and set aside.

For the Steak:

1. Slice flank steak against the grain into 1/4 inch slices with the knife held at a 45 degree angle. Some of the really long pieces I cut in half to make them more bite-sized.

2. Heat avocado oil in skillet over medium-high heat.

3. Add beef (may need to cook in 2 batches) and cook 2-3 minutes, until brown, flipping pieces over to cook both sides.

4. Add the sauce to the pan along with the xantham gum and cook over medium heat for a few minute, Stirring to coat meat.

5. Add green onions and remove from heat.

Keto Beef Stew

⏱ Cook Time: 1 hour 45 minutes	🍴 Serving:4					
🍳 Fat 14g	🍱 Carbogydrates:17g	☺	Protein:40g	©	Calories:35

Ingredients

- 2 lb. beef chuck roast, cut into 1" pieces
- Kosher salt
- Freshly ground black pepper
- 2 tbsp. extra-virgin olive oil
- 8 oz. Baby bella mushrooms, sliced
- 1 small onion, chopped
- 1 medium carrot, peeled and cut into rounds
- 2 stalks celery, sliced
- 3 cloves garlic, minced
- 1 tbsp. tomato paste
- 6 c. low-sodium beef broth
- 1 tsp. fresh thyme leaves
- 1 tsp. freshly chopped rosemary

Instructions

1. Pat beef dry with paper towels and season well with salt and pepper. In a large pot over medium heat, heat oil. Working in batches, add beef and sear on

107

all sides until golden, about 3 minutes per side. Remove from pot and repeat with remaining beef, adding more oil as necessary.

2. To same pot, add mushrooms and cook until golden and crispy, 5 minutes. Add onion, carrots, and celery and cook until soft, 5 minutes. Add garlic and cook until fragrant, 1 minute more. Add tomato paste and and stir to coat vegetables.

3. Add broth, thyme, rosemary, and beef to pot and season with salt and pepper. Bring to a boil and reduce heat to a simmer. Simmer until beef is tender, 50 minutes to an hour.

Aromatic Diced Beef

⏱ Cook Time: 30 min	🍴 Serving:2				
🍲 Fat 30g	🍰 Carbogydrates:10g	☺ Protein:51g	© Calories:504		

Ingredients

- 450 g good quality diced beef
- 130 g fresh cherry tomatoes, cut in half
- 30 g shallots, finely chopped
- 1 medium-sized green chilli pepper
- 1 tbsp coconut oil (measured solid)
- 2 tbsp olive oil
- 1 tsp cumin
- 1 tsp coriander seeds
- 1 tsp black mustard seeds
- 1 piece of star anise
- 1 tsp freshly ground black pepper
- 1/2 tsp salt
- a pinch of nutmeg
- water

Instructions

1. Heat the coconut oil and 1 tbsp of olive oil in a pan.

2. Prepare all the spices in a mortar (freshly ground spices allow you to create a dish that is more aromatic). Leave the piece of star anise as it is and don't add the salt yet.

3. Add the finely chopped shallots in the pan and stir until translucent.

109

4. Add the spices and stir until fragrant.

5. Add the meat (dry the diced beef with some paper towel first) and stir until fully browned on the outside.

6. Add the chopped tomatoes and green chilli pepper.

7. Add enough water to cover all the ingredients and reduce the heat. Let simmer for approx. 20 minutes. Add more water if necessary but keep in mind that the final result should have just a bit of creamy (not watery) sauce around the meat.

8. When the dish is ready, remove the piece of star anise and add the salt and the remaining tablespoon of olive oil. Taste and adjust the amount of spices and salt if necessary. Serve warm with finely chopped spring onions or parsley on top.

Meatloaf Recipe

⏱	Cook Time: 70 min	🍴	Serving:4				
🥩	Fat 44g	🍞	Carbogydrates:5g	☺	Protein:35g	©	Calories:579

Ingredients

- 1 tablespoon tallow
- 1 small onion finely chopped
- 2 cloves garlic crushed
- 2 pounds ground beef
- 2 large eggs
- 2 tablespoons oregano dried
- 1 1/2 teaspoon salt
- 1/4 teaspoon pepper ground
- 1/3 cup low carb marinara sauce
- 1/3 cup almond flour
- 2 tablespoons low carb marinara sauce extra

Instructions

1. Preheat your oven to 160C/320F and prepare a loaf tin by lining with baking paper.

2. Place a non-stick frying pan over high heat and saute the onion and garlic in the tallow, until the onion is turning translucent. Set aside to cool slightly.

3. In a large mixing bowl add the warm onion mixture and all remaining ingredients, except the extra marinara sauce.

4. Using clean hands, or wearing disposable gloves, mix the ingredients very well.

5. Press into the base of your prepared loaf tin, ensuring there are no air bubbles, and smooth the top.

6. Bake for 50 minutes.

7. Drain off some of the juices and top the meatloaf with the extra marinara sauce.

8. Bake for another 10 minutes.

9. Leave to sit for 10 minutes to rest, before slicing and serving.

Moroccan Meatballs

⏱	Cook Time: 6 hours	🍳	Serving:8				
🥩	Fat 27g	🍰	Carbogydrates:6g	💧 Protein:22g	©	Calories:363

Ingredients

- 2 pounds of Ground Beef
- 1 small Onion, grated
- 4 cloves of Garlic, crushed
- 1 large Egg
- 2 tablespoons of Cilantro, finely chopped
- 1 tablespoon of Cumin, ground
- 1 tablespoon of Coriander, ground
- 1 tablespoon of Smoked Paprika, ground
- 2 teaspoons of Ground Ginger
- 1 teaspoon of Cinnamon, ground
- 1 teaspoon of Salt
- 2 tablespoon of Olive Oil
- 2 tablespoons of Tomato Paste
- 1 ½ cups of Tomato Passata
- ½ cup of Beef Stock
- ⅓ cup of Cilantro, to serve

Instructions

1. In a large bowl add the beef, half the grated onion, half the garlic, egg, cilantro, cumin, coriander, paprika, ginger, cinnamon, and salt. Mix well.

2. Roll into 2 tablespoon-sized meatballs and set aside. We got 40.

113

3. Place the oil, remaining onion, and garlic into a nonstick frying pan over high heat. Saute for 3-5 minutes, until fragrant.

4. Add the tomato paste and cook for another 3 minutes, then add to your slow cooker, followed by the passata and stock. Mix well.

5. Add the meatballs to the sauce.

6. Cook on low for 5 hours.

Low Carb Beef Bolognese Sauce

⏱	Cook Time: 1 hr 15 min	⚗	Serving:6			
🍲	Fat 21g	🍱	Carbogydrates:5g	😊 Protein:17g	©	Calories:279

Ingredients

- 4 cups of Beef Stock or Broth
- 2 ounces of Tallow
- 1 medium Onion, diced
- 6 cloves of Garlic, crushed
- 1 tablespoon of Marjoram, dried
- 1 teaspoon of Salt
- 3 pounds of Ground Beef
- 24 ounces of Tomato Puree
- 1 teaspoon of Pepper
- 2 tablespoons of Basil, chopped
- 2 tablespoons of Oregano, chopped
- 1 tablespoon of Parsley, chopped

Instructions

1. Place the beef stock into a small saucepan and simmer over medium-high heat until it reduces into 1 cup of liquid.

2. In a large saucepan over high heat, place the tallow and allow to melt and heat.

3. Add the diced onion, garlic, marjoram, and salt. Saute for 5 minutes, until the onions have softened and turned translucent.

115

4. Add the ground beef and saute until browned. Reduce the heat to low.

5. Pour in the tomato puree and reduced beef stock and simmer, uncovered, and stirring occasionally for 30-60 minutes. Until the liquid is mostly absorbed, leaving a thick and rich sauce.

6. Add the remaining ingredients, check the seasoning, and add more salt or pepper if desired.

7. Remove from the heat, serve, and enjoy.

Keto Lamb Curry

⏱ Cook Time: 2 hr 35 min	🍳 Serving:8				
🍖 Fat 17g	🥖 Carbogydrates:2g	💧 Protein:30g	© Calories:480		

Ingredients

Marinade

- 2 teaspoons of Ginger, crushed
- 3 cloves of Garlic, crushed
- 2 teaspoons of Cumin, ground
- 2 teaspoons of Coriander, ground
- 1 teaspoon of Onion Powder
- 1 teaspoon of Cardamon, ground
- 1 teaspoon of Paprika, ground
- 1 teaspoon of Turmeric, ground
- 1 teaspoon of Kashmiri Chili Powder
- 2 tablespoons of Olive Oil

Curry

- 4 pounds of Lamb Shoulder, diced
- 3 tablespoons of Ghee
- 1 medium Onion, diced
- 1 teaspoon of Cinnamon, ground
- 1 teaspoon of Kashmiri Chili Powder
- 2 teaspoons of Salt
- 1 teaspoon of Pepper
- 1 cup of Heavy Cream
- ½ cup of Flaked Almonds
- 3 tablespoons of Cilantro, roughly chopped

Instructions

1. The Marinade: In a mixing bowl combine all marinade ingredients.

117

2. Add the diced lamb and mix well.

3. Store in the fridge to marinate for at least 1 hour, or overnight.

4. The Curry: In a large saucepan add the ghee and place over medium heat.

5. Add the onion, cinnamon & chili powder and saute for 3 minutes.

6. Add the marinated lamb, salt, and pepper and stir to ensure that lamb is browning.

7. Allow the lamb to cook for 10 minutes before adding the cream and reducing the heat to low.

8. Simmer the curry, partially covered, for 1 hour. Check the lamb for tenderness. If the lamb is tough, continue cooking until tender.

9. Remove the lid and simmer for another 10 minutes.

10. Add the flaked almonds and stir well. Add any extra seasoning.

11. Remove from the heat, garnish with coriander and serve.

Rosemary Dijon Roasted Lamb Chops

⏱ Cook Time: 17 min	🍖 Serving:4			
🍞 Fat 40g	🚗 Carbogydrates:2g	◔ Protein:18g	© Calories:446

Ingredients

- 1 tbsp Dijon mustard
- 2 cloves garlic minced
- 3 tbsp olive oil
- 2 tsp fresh rosemary finely chopped
- 1/2 tsp salt
- 1/4 tsp pepper
- 4 lamb loin chops aprrox 2 lbs with bone-in

Instructions

1. Whisk together Dijon mustard, garlic, olive oil, rosemary, and salt and pepper in a bowl. Place lamb chops in a large zip-top bag or other airtight container. Coat lamb with Dijon mixture on both sides. Let marinate in the fridge for at least 30 minutes, but up to 24 hours.

2. Position an oven rack to the highest position in the oven and line a broiler pan with aluminum foil.

3. Take lamb chops out of the bag and place onto prepared pan. Set oven to broil on high and place pan into the oven.

4. Cook lamb chops for 8 minutes, until brown, and then flip and cook for an additional 3-5 minutes depending on the doneness you like your meat. (3 minutes for medium rare, 4 for medium, 5 for well done)

Keto Lamb Chops on the Grill

⏱ Cook Time: 8 hr 17 min	🐑 Serving:8			
🍖 Fat 27g	🍰 Carbogydrates:1g	☺ Protein:17g	© Calories:446

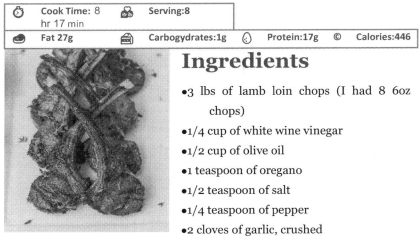

Ingredients

- 3 lbs of lamb loin chops (I had 8 6oz chops)
- 1/4 cup of white wine vinegar
- 1/2 cup of olive oil
- 1 teaspoon of oregano
- 1/2 teaspoon of salt
- 1/4 teaspoon of pepper
- 2 cloves of garlic, crushed
- zest of 1 lemon
- juice of 2 lemons (approx. 6 tablespoons)

Instructions

1. Whisk together all of the marinade ingredinets. Add the chops to a large baggie and pour the marinade over top.

2. Seal the bag and use your hands to mix the marinade through the chops and then place in the refrigerator for 8 hours or overnight.

3. Take out the lamb chops when ready to eat and let them sit on the ccounter for 15 minutes. Place them on a plate and discard the marinade.

4. Grill the lamb chops for about 5-6 minutes per side. The time will depend on the size and thickness of the chops. Mine were about 1 - 1.5 inches thick and too 6 minutes on each side and came out medium rare.

Braised Lamb Shanks

⏱ Cook Time: 3 hr 30 min	🍴 Serving:4				
🍖 Fat 10g	🥘 Carbogydrates:15g	🥄 Protein:44g	© Calories:334		

Ingredients

- 4 cloves garlic minced
- 1 cup finely diced carrot
- 1 cup finely diced celery
- 1/3 cup balsamic vinegar
- 3 tbsp tomato paste
- 3 cups beef stock
- 2 bay leaves
- 1 tsp dried thyme
- 1/4 tsp pepper
- 1/4 tsp salt

- 4 lamb shanks
- 1 tbsp olive oil
- 1 onion finely diced

Instructions

1. Preheat the oven to 350° Fahrenheit (175° Celsius)
2. Season the lamb shanks on all sides with salt and pepper. Heat 1 tbsp oil in a large pan on medium high heat and sear the shanks on all sides (approx 8 minutes). Once seared, set aside on a plate.
3. Add the garlic, onion, celery and carrot to the pan and saute for 5 minutes until the vegetables begin to soften.
4. Add the balsamic vinegar, tomato paste, beef stock, thyme, bay leaves, salt and pepper to the pan and give everything a stir. Bring to a gentle simmer. Once simmering return the lamb shanks to the pan and spoon some of the sauce overtop. Cover with a lid and cook in the oven for an 1 1/2 hours.
5. After 1 1/2 hours of cooking, flip the shanks over and return to the oven to cook for 1 more hour, but with the lid off (this will brown the shanks and help the sauce to thicken).

6. After a total of 2 1/2 hours in the oven, the lamb shanks should be fall apart tender. Serve them with veggies or mash and lots of the sauce poured overtop.

Keto Lamb Koftas

⏱	Cook Time: 20 min	🍴	Serving:4				
🍖	Fat 26g	🍞	Carbogydrates:3g	🍰	Protein:22g	©	Calories:330

Ingredients

- 500 g minced (ground) lamb (1.1 lb)
- 1 garlic clove, minced
- 1/2 medium yellow onion, diced (50 g/ 1.8 oz)
- 1 tsp dried oregano
- 2 tbsp chopped fresh parsley
- 1/2 tsp sea salt
- 1/4 tsp ground black pepper
- 1 tbsp extra virgin olive oil (15 ml)

Instructions

1. Place your skewers in cold water for half and hour prior to starting (ideally leave them to soak for at least 30 minutes). Alternatively, you can use stainless steel skewers that don't require soaking.
2. Add minced lamb, diced onions, chopped garlic, finely chopped parsley and the herbs and seasonings into a large mixing bowl. Retain the olive oil.
3. Mix well with your hands until thoroughly combined.
4. Portion out into eight portions and place each one around a skewer. You need to gently squeeze and press your mixture around the skewer until you're happy with the result. If your skewers will fit in a pan, heat it on the stove top. Mine were too big so I cooked them on our barbeque instead.
5. Brush the surface with the retained olive oil before placing the koftas onto the hot pan.

6. Store the koftas in the refrigerator, covered for 4 days.

Greek Lamb and Cabbage Bowls

⏱ Cook Time: 20 min		👥 Serving:4			
🍲 Fat 10g	🍱	Carbogydrates:15g	😊 Protein:34g	©	Calories:334

Ingredients

- 1 small onion, diced
- 1 lb grass-fed ground lamb
- ¼ cup tomato paste
- 1 teaspoon ground cinnamon
- ½ teaspoon dried oregano
- ¼ teaspoon ground nutmeg
- ½ cup water (or broth), more or less as needed
- ½ large head green cabbage (or 1 small), cored and sliced
- 1 teaspoon sea salt and ½ teaspoon black pepper, or to taste
- 1 tablespoon olive oil
- 1 large clove garlic, minced

Instructions

1. In a large pan, dutch oven or skillet, heat the olive oil over medium-high heat. Add the onion, garlic and ground lamb. Sauté until the lamb is cooked about 5- 7 minutes.
2. Add in the tomato paste, cinnamon, oregano and nutmeg. Stir until well combined.
3. Add in the cabbage and continue to sauté. You want to cook until the cabbage is gently cooked with a little bite, not mushy.
4. Add a little water or broth, as needed if it's too dry.
5. Serve over cauli-rice or rice, zucchini noodles or pasta.

Lamb Meatballs with Mint Gremolata

⏱ Cook Time: 20 min	⚙ Serving:4			
🍖 Fat 17g	🍱 Carbogydrates:4g	💧 Protein:34g	© Calories:306	

Ingredients

For the meatballs:

- 2 lbs ground lamb
- 2 eggs
- 1/2 cup superfine almond flour **
- 1/4 cup fresh parsley, chopped
- 1 clove garlic, minced
- 1 1/2 Tbsp Za'atar seasoning
- 1 tsp kosher salt
- 3 Tbsp water
- 2 Tbsp olive oil for frying

For the gremolata:

- 2 Tbsp chopped fresh parsley
- 2 Tbsp chopped fresh mint
- 1 Tbsp lime zest
- 2 cloves garlic, minced

Instructions

For the meatballs:

1. Combine the meatball ingredients (except olive oil) in a medium bowl and mix well.
2. Form into 24 one and a half inch (approximately) meatballs.
3. Heat the olive oil in a nonstick saute pan over medium heat.
4. Cook the meatballs in batches until brown on both sides and cooked through – about 2-3 minutes per side.

5. Remove cooked meatballs and place on a paper towel lined plate until ready to serve.

6. Serve warm, sprinkled generously with gremolata.

For the gremolata:

7. Combine the ingredients in a small bowl and mix well.

Pecan Crusted Rack of Lamb

⏱	Cook Time: 40 min	🐣	Serving:3				
🍖	Fat 17g	🏦	Carbogydrates:8g	😋 Protein:34g	© Calories:336

Ingredients

- 1 rack of lamb (I used a pre-marinated garlic and rosemary rack; if using an unseasoned rack, add an extra clove of finely chopped garlic, and 1 tsp dried rosemary)
- 2 tbsp ghee
- 1/2 small onion (finely chopped)
- 1 tbsp yellow mustard
- 1 cup pecans (coarsely ground)
- 1–2 cloves garlic (finely chopped)
- zest of 1 lime
- salt and pepper to taste

Instructions

For the meatballs:

1. Remove lamb from refrigerator and allow to warm to room temperature (1-2 hrs).
2. Preheat oven to 400F.
3. Score the fat with a sharp knife and rub in salt and pepper.
4. Bake on a roasting tray for 10 minutes then remove from oven.
5. In the meantime, saute onions in ghee over medium heat in a small frying pan.

6. When onions are soft add garlic, pecans, and zest (and rosemary if adding) and stir well.

7. Cover lamb in mustard, then coat in pecan mix (easiest to use your hands – careful: it's hot).

8. Return to oven on roasting tray for 20-30 minutes – use a meat thermometer (remove just prior to desired doneness – it will continue to cook).

9. Let meat rest a few minutes before cutting between ribs into individual cutlets.

Vegetable Dishes

Snap Pea Salad

⏱ Cook Time: 40 min	🍤 Serving:4			
🍖 Fat 20g	🧀 Carbogydrates:6g	😊 Protein:4g	© Calories:212	

Ingredients

- 8 ounces cauliflower riced
- 1/4 cup lemon juice
- 1/4 cup olive oil
- 1 clove garlic crushed
- 1/2 teaspoon coarse grain dijon mustard
- 1 teaspoon granulated stevia/erythritol blend
- 1/4 teaspoon pepper
- 1/2 teaspoon sea salt
- 1/2 cup sugar snap peas ends removed and each pod cut into three pieces
- 1/4 cup chives
- 1/2 cup sliced almonds
- 1/4 cup red onions minced

Instructions

1. Pour 1 to 2 inches of water in a pot fitted with a steamer. Bring water to a simmer.

2. Place riced cauliflower in the steamer basket, sprinkle lightly with sea salt, cover, and place over the simmering water in the bottom of the steamer. Steam until tender, about 10-12 minutes.

3. When cauliflower is tender, remove the top of the steamer from the simmering water and place it over a bowl, so any excess water can drain out. Allow to cool, uncovered for about 10 minutes, then cover and place the steamer and the bowl in the refrigerator. Chill for at least 1/2 hour or until cool to the touch.

4. While cauliflower is cooling, make the dressing. Pour olive oil in a small mixing bowl. Gradually stream in the lemon juice while vigorously whisking. Whisk in the garlic, mustard, sweetener, pepper, and salt.

5. In a medium mixing bowl, combine chilled cauliflower, peas, chives, almonds, and red onions. Pour dressing over and stir to mix. Transfer to an airtight container and refrigerate until serving. This salad is best if it is allowed to sit for a few hours in the refrigerator so the flavors mingle.

Garlic & Chive Cauliflower Mash

⏱ Cook Time: 20 min	🍴 Serving:2				
🍛 Fat 18g	🍞 Carbogydrates:3g	☺ Protein:2g	© Calories:178

Ingredients

- 4 cups cauliflower florets
- 1/3 cup mayonnaise
- 1 clove garlic, peeled
- 1 Tbsp water
- 1/2 tsp Kosher salt
- 1/8 tsp black pepper
- 1/4 tsp lemon juice
- 1/2 tsp lemon (or lime) zest
- 1 Tbsp fresh chives, chopped

Instructions

1. Combine the cauliflower, mayonnaise, garlic, water, salt and pepper in a large microwave safe bowl, stirring to coat.

2. Microwave on high for 12-15 minutes (or longer), until completely softened.

3. Add the cooked mixture to a magic bullet or food processor and puree until smooth.

4. Add the lemon juice, zest and chives and pulse until combined.

5. Serve warm.

Creamy Cilantro Lime Coleslaw

⏱	Cook Time: 10 min	🐾	Serving:5				
🍲	Fat 8.9g	🍰	Carbogydrates:9g	(:)	Protein:3.2g	©	Calories:119

Ingredients

- 14 oz coleslaw, bagged
- 1 1/2 avocados
- 1/4 cup cilantro leaves
- 2 limes, juiced
- 1 garlic clove
- 1/4 cup water
- 1/2 teaspoon salt
- cilantro to garnish

Instructions

1. In a food processor add the garlic and cilantro and process until chopped.
2. Add the lime juice, avocados and water. Pulse until nice and creamy.
3. Take out the avocado mixture and in a large bowl mix it with the coleslaw. It will be a bit thick but it will cover the slaw nicely.
4. For best results, refrigerate for a few hours before eating to soften the cabbage.

Cauliflower Hummus

⏱ Cook Time: 20 min	🐌 Serving:1					
🍖 Fat 14g	🍰 Carbogydrates:3.5g	☺ Protein:2g	© Calories:119			

Ingredients

- 3 cups raw cauliflower florets
- 2 Tbsp water
- 2 Tbsp avocado or olive oil
- 1/2 tsp salt
- 3 whole garlic cloves
- Tbsp Tahini paste
- 3 Tbsp lemon juice
- 2 raw garlic cloves, crushed (in addition to above)
- 3 Tbsp extra virgin olive oil
- 3/4 tsp kosher salt
- smoked paprika and extra olive oil for serving

Instructions

1. Combine the cauliflower, water, 2 Tbsp avocado or olive oil, 1/2 tsp kosher salt, and 3 whole garlic cloves to a microwave safe dish. Microwave for about 15 minutes – or until softened and darkened in color.
2. Put the cauliflower mixture into a magic bullet, blender, or food processor and blend. Add the tahini paste, lemon juice, 2 raw garlic cloves, 3 Tbsp olive oil, and 3/4 tsp kosher salt. Blend until mostly smooth. Taste and adjust seasoning as necessary.
3. To serve, place the hummus in a bowl and drizzle with extra virgin olive oil and a sprinkle of paprika. Use thinly sliced tart apples, celery sticks, raw radish chips, or other vegges to dip with.

Crispy Tofu and Bok Choy Salad

⏱ Cook Time: 40 min	🍴 Serving:3		
🍲 Fat 6g	🍱 Carbogydrates:9g	© Protein:24g	© Calories:398

Ingredients

Oven
Baked
Tofu

•15

ounces extra firm tofu

•1 tablespoon soy sauce

•1 tablespoon sesame oil

•1 tablespoon water

•2 teaspoons minced garlic

•1 tablespoon rice wine vinegar

•Juice ½ lemon

Bok Choy Salad

•9 ounces bok choy

•1 stalk green onion

•2 tablespoons chopped cilantro

•3 tablespoons coconut oil

•2 tablespoons soy sauce

•1 tablespoon sambal olek

•1 tablespoon peanut butter

•Juice ½ lime

•7 drops liquid stevia

Instructions

1. Start by pressing the tofu. Lay the tofu in a kitchen towel and put something heavy over the top (like a cast iron skillet). It takes about 4-6 hours to dry out, and you may need to replace the kitchen towel half-way through.

2. Once the tofu is pressed, work on your marinade. Combine all of the ingredients for the marinade (soy sauce, sesame oil, water, garlic, vinegar, and lemon).

3. Chop the tofu into squares and place in a plastic bag along with the marinade. Let this marinate for at least 30 minutes, but preferably over night.

133

4. Pre-heat oven to 350°F. Place tofu on a baking sheet lined with parchment paper (or a silpat) and bake for 30-35 minutes.

5. As the tofu is cooked, get started on the bok choy salad. Chop cilantro and spring onion.

6. Mix all of the other ingredients together (except lime juice and bok choy) in a bowl. Then add cilantro and spring onion. Note: You can microwave coconut oil for 10-15 seconds to allow it it to melt.

7. Once the tofu is almost cooked, add lime juice into the salad dressing and mix together.

8. Chop the bok choy into small slices, like you would cabbage.

9. Remove the tofu from the oven and assemble your salad with tofu, bok choy, and sauce. Enjoy!

Vegan Kale and Spinach Soup

⏱ Cook Time: 15 min	🍽 Serving:4				
🍲 Fat 12g	🏺 Carbogydrates:6g	🥄 Protein:4g	© Calories:108

Ingredients

- ½ cup coconut oil, melted
- 8 oz. kale
- 8 oz. (7½ cups) fresh spinach
- 2 (14 oz.) avocados
- 3½ cups coconut milk or coconut cream
- 1 cup water
- fresh mint or dried mint (optional)
- 1 tsp salt
- ¼ tsp ground black pepper
- 1 tbsp lime juice

Fried kale

- 3 oz. kale
- 2 garlic cloves, chopped
- 2 tbsp coconut oil
- ½ tsp ground cardamom (green)

salt and pepper

Instructions

1. Melt the coconut oil in a hot thick-bottomed pot or pan.
2. Sauté the spinach and kale briefly. The vegetable should just shrink and get a little color, but no more. Remove from the heat.
3. Add water, coconut milk, avocado and spices. Blend with a hand blender until creamy.
4. Add lime juice. Add more spices if you want.
5. Fry kale and garlic on high heat until the garlic turns golden. Garnish the soup and serve.

Carrot Salad

⏱ Cook Time: 15 min	🦀 Serving:4		
🍥 Fat 8g	🍰 Carbogydrates:12g	© Protein:4g	© Calories:92

Ingredients

- 1 pound carrots, julienned
- 3 Medjool dates, pitted and diced
- ¼ cup chopped pistachios
- ⅓ cup finely chopped cilantro
- ¼ cup mint leaves, optional

Dressing

- 2 tablespoons extra-virgin olive oil
- 2 tablespoons fresh lemon juice
- 1 tablespoon tahini
- 1 tablespoon honey
- 1 small garlic clove, grated
- ¼ teaspoon cumin
- ¼ teaspoon sea salt

Instructions

1. Place the julienned carrots in a large bowl and sprinkle the dates on top.
2. Make the dressing: In a small bowl, whisk together the olive oil, lemon juice, tahini, honey, garlic, cumin, and salt.
3. Drizzle the dressing over the carrots and toss to coat. Sprinkle on the pistachios and cilantro and toss again. Sprinkle the mint leaves and serve.

Cabbage Soup

⏱	Cook Time: 35 min	👥	Serving:6				
🍲	Fat 8g	🏠	Carbogydrates:16g	😊	Protein:8g	©	Calories:112

Ingredients

- 2 tablespoons extra-virgin olive oil
- 2 carrots, chopped
- 1 medium yellow onion, diced
- 1 celery rib, diced
- 2 tablespoons white wine vinegar
- 2 (14.5-ounce) cans fire roasted diced tomatoes
- 4 cups vegetable broth
- 1 (15.5-ounce) can cooked white beans, drained and rinsed
- 4 garlic cloves, grated
- 2 Yukon gold potatoes, diced
- 1 small green cabbage, about 1 pound (9 cups chopped)
- 1 teaspoon dried thyme
- ¾ teaspoon sea salt
- Freshly ground black pepper
- Fresh parsley, for garnish

Instructions

1. Heat the oil in a large pot over medium heat. Add the carrots, onion, celery, salt, and several grinds of fresh pepper, and cook, stirring occasionally, for 8 minutes.
2. Add the vinegar, stir, and then add the tomatoes, broth, beans, garlic, potatoes, cabbage and thyme. Cover and simmer for 20 to 30 minutes, or until the potatoes and cabbage are tender.

3. Season to taste, garnish with fresh parsley, and serve.

Creamy Dairy Free Avocado Sauce

⏱ Cook Time: 20 min	🍽 Serving:1				
🍖 Fat 16g	🍰 Carbogydrates:8g	🥚 Protein:6g	© Calories:180		

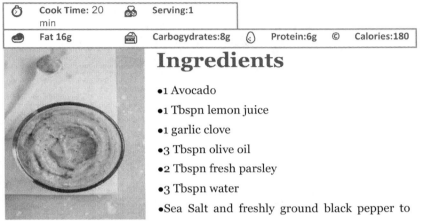

Ingredients

- 1 Avocado
- 1 Tbspn lemon juice
- 1 garlic clove
- 3 Tbspn olive oil
- 2 Tbspn fresh parsley
- 3 Tbspn water
- Sea Salt and freshly ground black pepper to taste

Instructions

1. Add all ingredients into food processor or blender.
2. Blend until smooth.
3. Add more water to reach a thinner consistency if desired.
4. Taste and adjust seasoning if necessary.

Easy No-Churn Avocado Ice Cream

⏱ Cook Time: 5 hours	🐾 Serving:4				
🍖 Fat 17g	🍱 Carbogydrates:29g	☺ Protein:3g	© Calories:274		

Ingredients

- 1/4 cup hardened coconut cream (from 1 14-oz can full-fat coconut milk, refrigerated overnight — only the cream)
- 2 ripe avocados, halved, pitted and peeled
- 2 very ripe bananas, sliced and frozen
- 3 tbsp pure maple syrup, plus more, to taste
- 1 tbsp freshly squeezed lemon juice

Instructions

1. Add sliced, peeled fresh avocado to a food processor or high-speed blender, and blend until smooth.

2. Add hardened coconut cream from canned coconut milk, along with sliced frozen bananas, pure maple syrup, and lemon juice, and blend until smooth and creamy. If bananas are not fully ripe, you may need to add in additional maple syrup.

3. Taste, and add any more pure maple syrup, as needed, to reach the desired sweetness.

4. Transfer the mixture into a freezer-safe container, and place in freezer for at least 3-4 hours or overnight.

5. When ready to serve, let soften for 10-15 minutes at room temperature before scooping.

Arugula Avocado Tomato Salad

⏱ Cook Time: 20 min	🍳 Serving:1				
🍖 Fat9g	🍰 Carbogydrates:12g	😊 Protein:3g	© Calories:112		

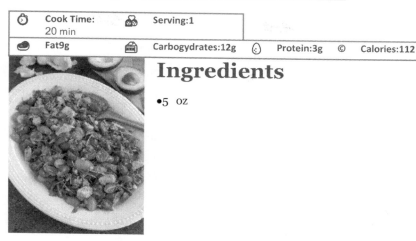

Ingredients

- 5 oz baby arugula roughly chopped
- 6 large basil leaves thinly sliced
- 1 pint yellow grape tomatoes sliced in half
- 1 pint red grape tomatoes sliced in half
- 2 large avocados cut into chunks
- ½ cup red onion minced
- Balsamic Vinaigrette
- 2 tbsp balsamic vinegar
- 1 tbsp olive oil
- 1 tbsp maple syrup
- 1 tbsp lemon juice
- 1 small garlic clove minced
- ¼ tsp himalayan pink sea salt
- ¼ tsp black pepper

Instructions

1. Put the roughly chopped arugula and sliced basil leaves into a large mixing bowl. Add the sliced grape tomatoes, avocado chunks, and minced red onion to the bowl. Toss to combine.

2. In a small bowl, whisk together 2 tbsp balsamic vinegar, 1 tbsp olive oil, 1 tbsp maple syrup, 1 tbsp lemon juice, 1 garlic clove, ¼ tsp salt, and ¼ tsp black pepper until well combined.

3. Pour the balsamic dressing over the salad. Gently mix the salad until the dressing has been evenly distributed and then transfer the salad to a large platter.

Red Curry Cauliflower Soup

⏱ Cook Time: 45 min	🍴 Serving:6				
🍲 Fat 16g	🍱 Carbogydrates:18g	🥄 Protein:6g	© Calories:274

Ingredients

- 1 medium yellow onion sliced
- 3 medium garlic cloves sliced
- 4 ounces thai red curry paste (about 4 tbsp)
- 1 medium cauliflower (about 1 lb cauliflower florets)
- ½ cup red lentils
- 1 ½ cups water
- 4 cups low-sodium vegetable broth
- ½ tsp Himalayan pink sea salt
- ½ tsp black pepper
- 14 ounce can unsweetened coconut milk
- 3 tbsp lemon juice (1 large lemon)
- 1 tbsp chives sliced

Instructions

Vegan Keto Coconut Curry

⏱ Cook Time: 35 min	⚙ Serving:4			
🍲 Fat 33g	🍱 Carbogydrates:10g	☺ Protein:18g	© Calories:425

Ingredients

- ¼ cup vegan butter
- ½ green bell pepper, thinly sliced
- 2 scallions, thinly sliced, white and green parts kept separate
- 2 garlic cloves, thinly sliced
- 2½ tablespoons vegan red curry paste
- 1 medium zucchini, diced
- 1 medium carrot, diced
- 1½ cups unsweetened full-fat coconut milk
- 1 cup vegetable stock
- 2 tablespoons unflavored vegan protein powder
- 2 tablespoons natural unsweetened peanut butter
- 4 drops liquid stevia
- 1 teaspoon sea salt
- Freshly ground black pepper
- 16 ounces extra-firm tofu, cut into medium dice
- 1 cup baby spinach
- ¼ cup chopped fresh cilantro, plus more for serving
- 4 tablespoons coconut oil, melted

Instructions

1. In a large pot, melt the butter over medium heat. Add the bell pepper, scallion whites and garlic; cook until fragrant, about 1 minute. Add the curry paste and cook, stirring constantly, until fragrant, about 1 minute.

2. Stir in the zucchini, carrot, coconut milk, vegetable stock, protein powder, peanut butter, stevia, salt and black pepper. Bring to a boil,

145

then reduce the heat to medium-low and simmer uncovered until the vegetables are tender, 8 to 10 minutes. Taste and adjust the seasoning if necessary.

3. Add the tofu and simmer for 5 minutes to warm through. Add the spinach and cilantro to wilt. Taste and adjust the seasoning if necessary.

4. Divide the curry among four bowls. Drizzle 1 tablespoon melted coconut oil over each portion. Sprinkle with the scallion greens and more cilantro.

Keto Apple Crisp

⏱ Cook Time: 1 hours 5 min	🍴 Serving:8				
🍲 Fat: 13g	🍱 Carbogydrates:6g	🥄 Protein:3g	© Calories:138		

Ingredients

FILLING:

- •6 cups zucchini peeled and sliced
- •3 tablespoons lemon juice can sub half with apple cider vinegar to add apple flavor
- •⅔ cup low carb sugar substitute or 4 Tbsp 2 tsp Truvia
- •¾ teaspoon ground cinnamon
- •½ teaspoon ground nutmeg
- •¼ teaspoon xanthan gum optional thickener
- •1 teaspoon apple extract optional

TOPPING:

- •½ cup pecans chopped
- •½ cup almond flour
- •¼ cup oat fiber or coconut flour
- •¼ cup low carb sugar substitute or brown sugar substitute
- •1 teaspoon cinnamon
- •¼ cup butter

Instructions

1. In medium bowl, combine zucchini, lemon juice, sweetener, cinnamon and nutmeg until well blended. For a stronger apple taste, stir in apple extract too. Pour mixture into a greased 9 x 9-in. baking dish.
2. For topping, combine pecans, almond flour, oat fiber, sweetener and cinnamon in a bowl then cut in butter until crumbly. Sprinkle over the zucchini mixture.
3. Bake at 350 F for 45-50 minutes or until zucchini is tender.

147

Conclusion

Dear friends, I hope that the recipes you find in this book are interesting and useful. I am sure that the main success of any diet is to believe in yourself and not give up in the face of difficulties.

Be healthy and happy!

Always yours Sandra Grant.

Made in the USA
Coppell, TX
18 May 2022